HOLD NOTHING BACK!

HOLD NOTHING BACK!

HOW SACRIFICIAL OBEDIENCE LEADS TO INTIMACY WITH GOD

Alicia Williamson

New Hope Publishers

Birmingham, Alabama

New Hope Publishers
P. O. Box 12065
Birmingham, AL 35202-2065
www.newhopepubl.com

Library of Congress Cataloging-in-Publication Data
Williamson, Alicia, 1965–
    Hold nothing back! : how sacrificial obedience leads to intimacy with
God / by Alicia Williamson.
        p. cm.
    ISBN 1-56309-742-7 (pbk.)
    1. Sacrifice—Christianity. I. Title.
    BT265.3 .W55 2002
    248.4—dc21

                                                    2002010475

Cover design by Righteous Planet, Nashville, Tennessee

ISBN: 1-56309-742-7
N034105• 1002 • 5M1

Dedication

I would like to dedicate this book to my husband Richard, who gives sacrificially of himself and all he has to me and our boys, day in and day out. I also dedicate this to my sons, Michael Chandler and Richard David, whose lives have already taught me the value and rich reward of sacrifice and dying daily to myself. To my parents: you have shown me by example the power in and joy that accompanies sacrificial living. And to Jesus my Lord, thank you for your words in John 12.

"Truly, truly, I say to you, unless a grain of wheat falls into the earth and dies, it remains alone; but if it dies, it bears much fruit. He who loves his life loses it, and he who hates his life in this world will keep it to life eternal."
John 12:24–25

Table of Contents

Treasures

One by one He took them from me,
All the things I valued most,
Until I was empty-handed;
Every glittering toy was lost.

And I walked earth's highways, grieving,
In my rags and poverty.
Till I heard His voice inviting,
"Lift those empty hands to Me!"

So I held my hands toward Heaven,
And He filled them with a store
Of His own transcendent riches
Till they could contain no more.

And at last I comprehended
With my stupid mind and dull,
That God COULD not pour His riches
Into hands already full!

—Martha Snell Nicholson

Introduction

*F*or once in my life I was ready early! I had on my cute little red dress with black velvet trim and matching black velvet shoes. I had my hair and nails done. My make-up seemed to go on perfectly that day, and I had even remembered to pack the right jewelry and my favorite perfume. I was looking pretty good and feeling mighty fine as I sat in the hotel lobby waiting for the driver, who was to escort my friends and me to the Brooklyn Tabernacle in New York City.

Though I was giddy with excitement that day, I thought I had better do some praying to get my heart ready for church. About that time, a car pulled up and a handsome—no, a *fine*-looking—young man sprang out from it and came into the hotel lobby. He reminded me of Magnum P.I. and I jokingly said to God, "God, my ship has finally come in, and I am right here at the port." I clearly remember knowing in my heart, without a doubt, that God was *not* laughing.

I rose from the chair where I was sitting and asked, "Are you Richard Garcia?" (I had read his name on my itinerary.)

"Yes," he responded.

"Hi. I'm Alicia Williamson. My bags are over there. If you will get them, I'll call my friends and we can make our way to the church."

This poor guy did not know what had hit him, and I guess it was too early in the morning for him to figure it out. I sashayed over to the house phone to call my friends.

"Connie, Richard Garcia is here and he is *fine looking!*"

Ring, ring. "Chuck, Richard Garcia is here and he is *fine looking!* You sit in the front seat. Connie and I will sit in the back. I'll size him up and see if he's married or dating. You help me keep the conversation going." Click!

Off we went to church. Not much talking on the way there, but I noticed how handsome this guy was, how nice and clean cut, and that there was *no wedding band!* That was a good enough start.

We were in church all day and were pretty tired when it was all over. Richard had been a perfect gentleman all day. Now I had only a few minutes to find out what I really wanted to know. From the back seat, passenger side—where I could see his facial expressions—I moved in on him like a vicious but sophisticated piranha.

His answers to my questions were exactly what I wanted to hear: he was the perfect age. He was not married and had never been married. He was not dating or even seeing anyone. He had no children. And he had a job! He had no strange diseases and was not an activist in any strange political or spiritual movements.

Later that evening we exchanged phone numbers. It was the beginning of a relationship that has thrived to this very day. After developing our friendship over eleven months, Richard flew from New York City to Nashville, Tennessee, where I was recording, and surprised me. On Valentine's Day, in the Old Hickory Restaurant at the Opryland Hotel, "Magnum" asked me to be his Valentine forever. On December 28, 1996, at the Brooklyn Taberna-cle in Brooklyn, New York, Alicia Renee Williamson became Mrs. Richard Garcia.

There is so much more to this beautiful story—such as our first kiss, which turned into seven kisses, on the sixth floor of the Crowne Plaza Hotel, where we looked out every window to see the city from each vantage point. But I'll save that story for my first romance novel.

We honeymooned for fourteen fabulous days in Hawaii and came home to a beautiful new house in Mobile, Alabama. During our first year of marriage we traveled to places like the Bahamas and the Holy Land. Richard accompanied me as I worked and toured with the Billy Graham Organization and Women of Faith. I thought I was living a fairy tale.

Life was wonderful. We had each other and a relation-ship with the Almighty God. What more could we desire? We both had great jobs and—best yet—we had our health, so that we could enjoy all that God was giving us. We lacked nothing. Our prayers had been answered and our dreams had come true far beyond anything we could have asked or imagined. We were loving life and were thankful for all that God had done.

Then, sudden disaster. God had blessed me with a won-derful life. So it came as a complete shock when not too long after my marriage my doctor announced, "Alicia, you have cervical cancer." I felt my life slipping away. Why would God ask me to give up all of this? Why would God ask me to give up my husband, my home, my hope, and the happiness I had known over the past year of my life? After all, He had given all of these good gifts to me. I was keenly aware of this and tried to be thankful.

I know that all good and perfect gifts come from God (James 1:17). I know that He does not withhold His goodness from the righteous (Psalm 84:11). I know that He gives us all things to enjoy (1 Tim. 6:17). But at that crisis point in my life, I thought God was taking away from me all that He had given.

One of my favorite passages of Scripture is Jeremiah 29:11–13: "'For I know the plans that I have for you,' declares the LORD, 'plans for welfare and not for calamity to give you a future and a hope. Then you will call upon Me and come and pray to Me, and I will listen to you. You will seek Me and find Me when you search for Me with all your heart.'"

I believe these verses. I have tried to live in the truth of these verses. I know that God's desire for me is for good and not for calamity. But I did not understand the devastating circumstances I was now facing. The possibility of losing everything came crashing into my life. All I could hear were the words, "Alicia, you are going to die soon."

Proverbs 3:25 tells us not to fear sudden disaster. But we all have fear. I am convinced that since the events of September 11, 2001, the citizens of the United States—and, I believe, the world—have been in a constant state of fear, even though God has told us not to fear.

God uses everything, even what we see as awful, including sickness and disease, to bring about something good. He can use horrible incidents and the worst things of life for good. He gives life to the lifeless and hope to the hopeless. He can also bring peace and healing to fearful hearts, for He is God and Lord of all.

> I am the LORD, and there is no other;
> Besides Me there is no God.
> I will gird you, though you have not known Me;
> That men may know from the rising to the setting of the sun
> That there is no one besides Me.
> I am the LORD, and there is no other,

The One forming light and creating darkness,
Causing well-being and creating calamity;
I am the LORD who does all these.
Isaiah 45:5–7

God causes, God allows, God is always in control!

When I was sick, I honestly tried not to fear. But fear gripped my heart and my mind. I knew I had to let go of "me" and of my agenda in order to follow God in total faith and obedience.

I had lost three friends to cancer. All were very close to my age. My mother-in-law, who had passed away before I met Richard, had also lost her life to cervical cancer nine months after her diagnosis. I knew I was not exempt. I knew that just as my friends had gone on to be with the Lord, this might have been my time to do the same. Yet somewhere in my heart I knew that I could trust that God had a plan greater than I could see.

These were difficult days for me. Nevertheless, on the morning when I said "Yes, Lord," true inner healing and intimacy with God began to take place in a way I had never known. (I describe this in detail in my book *A Seeking Heart: Rediscovering True Worship*, coauthored by Sarah Groves.)

TRAGEDY TO TRIUMPH

My friend Marilyn Meberg has taught me the importance of "being willing to be made willing." If nothing else, in the midst of my fear I was *willing to be made willing* to trust God completely, to hold nothing back, so that He might do in my life whatever He wanted.

I lay on the living room floor, which became my altar of sacrifice, and prayed:

"*Yes, Lord.* If the time that I have left with Richard is short, then Thy kingdom come. *Yes, Lord.* Thank You for this beautiful home and the good gifts I have enjoyed. Thank You for a loving family and friends. Help me redeem the time I have left. Help me live inwardly, though outwardly I am perishing. I trust You completely with my life, with my all. I have no control. You are sovereign. You control all things, even my life. *Yes, Lord.* I will hold nothing back. I trust You with it all. *Yes, Lord.*"

I became the sacrifice. I put my life on the altar. It was into my heart that the knife plunged. I died. My will, my agenda, my initiative were no more. In my heart of hearts, all was gone. There was no Richard, there were no children, no home, no friends, no family, no more singing, no more traveling. There would be no books, no more records, nothing! Nothing except the presence of Jesus! But was that enough? Could His power, His presence, His promise, His love and grace be enough for me?

I had no choice. If Jesus were truly the Lord, the Master of my life, then my only answer could be "Yes, Lord." And "Yes, Lord" it finally was.

How I thank God for His amazing grace, which enabled me to submit my will to Him that day. How I praise Him for His Word and His promise, which were all that I had to cling to. I shout glory to Him for the power of His awesome presence and the power of the Holy Spirit that enabled me to say "Yes, Lord."

God's presence was real to me that day. More real than breakfast with Richard, more powerful than the love of a husband. His presence brought more life to me than any child could ever bring. And knowing that He was at home within my "Yes, Lord" was nothing short of true victory.

That day I realized, in my head and in my heart, that my husband and my marriage were gifts from God, but that Jesus Christ is Lord. My children would be gifts from God, but Jesus Christ is Lord. The good things that we enjoy, the fellowship of believers we worship with—all these are gifts from God, but *Jesus is Lord!*

This means that my allegiance to Jesus must take precedence over every other relationship or priority I may have. If this alignment is out of order, then there is sin in my life, the sin of idolatry, and I am separated from God because of it.

Because Jesus is Lord and Master of my life, He allowed these circumstances so that I might not drift *from* allegiance to Him *to* dependence and co-dependence upon my husband and others around me. Now, with Jesus, there is no more hoping, wishing, or dreaming. Jesus has made all my dreams come true. When I want a glimpse of a perfect me, I look to His cross, and I am there, crucified with Christ, yet I live.

My days had been filled with me and my new life. I knew intimacy with the people and things that God had given me, but not with God Himself. Very often I found myself frustrated and even disappointed because of the temporal nature of these gifts. I am thankful that God loved me enough to get my attention, as difficult as it was, and bring me back into intimacy with Himself.

> And at last I comprehended
> With my stupid mind and dull,
> That God could not pour His riches
> Into hands already full!

My experience in dealing with the reality that I had cancer was one of my darkest times, but in that moment God enabled me to trust Him completely with my life. In the laying-down of my self and all the good things God had given to me, I sensed His presence in a new and powerful way.

You can experience God in that same powerful way. But to know God's richest blessings you must lay yourself on the altar, *holding nothing back*.

Chapter One

Portrait of a Sacrifice

Sacrifice is not a word we hear very often in church or use frequently in modern day verbiage. We may have heard that Jesus is the final sacrifice, but how and why is that relevant in our lives today?

Why would I take the time to write about holding nothing back and how obedient sacrifice leads to intimacy with God?

I am writing because I have seen women across this country and around the world defeated in their Christian lives because they have not learned the secret to intimacy with God. Women flock from conference to conference, purchase book after book, CDs, T-shirts, purses, Bible covers, and checks with Scripture verses on them, trying to find intimacy with God. We will even buy the centerpiece right off the table. We've felt the nearness of God in the meeting, and now we want to buy it and take it home.

Now I have absolutely nothing against conferences and Christian paraphernalia. I am thankful to God that you are reading this book. You might even have some of my CDs. I hope so! Tell your friends about them!

But let me tell you now, reading this book will not give you intimacy with God. I have written this book to lead you to His book, the Bible. Intimacy with God begins with knowing the Word of God.

Listening to every CD you have in your Christian music collection will not bring you intimacy with God. Music is a tool for our emotions. Music has been given to soften and open our hearts, but the Word of God has been given to fill our hearts and change our lives.

You won't necessarily find intimacy when you gather with others in a Christian environment. Yes, you may sense the awe of His presence—and I pray you do. But trust me on this one: intimacy is a person to person, face-to-face experience with God.

Christian leaders use various resources to lead you to the main source, God's Word. Intimacy comes when you speak face-to-face with God. God speaks to us through His Word. When you open your Bible, it is God who is speaking. Listen to Him with a heart to obey. There you will find true intimacy with a holy, living, and loving God.

Webster's dictionary defines *intimacy* as something that is most private and personal—something deep, thorough, close, and familiar. Exodus 33:9 and 11 say, "Whenever Moses entered the tent, the pillar of cloud would descend and stand at the entrance of the tent; and the LORD would speak with Moses. . . . Thus the LORD used to speak to Moses face-to-face, just as a man speaks to his friend."

Intimacy with God happens when we go to Him honestly, opening to God the secret place of our hearts, and look into His face, ready to hear from Him through His Word. As we listen to Him with a heart to obey, He covers us with His presence and speaks to us His words that are private and personal, deep and thorough, close and familiar. As His words penetrate your soul, you will experience Him speaking directly to you.

"The secret of the LORD is for those who fear Him, and He will make them know His covenant" (Psalm 25:14). The word *secret* in that verse can be translated *intimacy*. Intimacy with the Lord is for those who fear or reverence Him. We learn to reverence God when we see Him as holy and sovereign and give our lives to Him in total faith and obedience. Intimacy is not reserved for Christian leaders alone, but for those who fear God. That means you. If you have a holy, reverent fear of God, then intimacy with God is His desire for you. His Word says so.

THE ORIGIN OF SACRIFICE

Great! Intimacy with God is what you want. That is why you are reading this book. But where does the element of sacrifice come in? How does obedient sacrifice lead to intimacy with God?

A sacrifice is an offering or gift, often requiring giving up or letting go of something that is highly valued. I like the figurative definition of sacrifice, which is what we will be discussing throughout this book. In this way, sacrifice is defined as an offering of a life or that which sustains life. It is the giving of one thing for the sake of another. Often, sacrifice involves the substitutionary death of one for the life of another.

This type of sacrifice is seen in Genesis 3:21. Instead of sentencing Adam and Eve to physical death, God sacrificed animals and clothed or covered Adam and Eve with the skin of the animals. Many believe this animal sacrifice is symbolic of our Lord Jesus Christ and the great sacrifice He would make for all people on the cross.

Because Adam and Eve had chosen to accept God's provision for their sin, they were restored to fellowship and intimacy with God. I believe this to be true because of what I see in the following chapter. In chapter four of Genesis we see the sons of Adam and Eve bringing sacrifices to God. They had to learn this action from someone, and the only people on the earth were their parents, Adam and Eve.

We are told that Cain brought an offering of the fruit of the ground while Abel, his younger brother, brought the firstlings of his flock and of their fat portions. Verses four and five say that God had regard for Abel and his offering, but for Cain and his offering God had no regard.

Cain had no reverent fear of God, no desire to know Him intimately, so he brought to God what he thought was adequate, but not what God had required. Cain's offering was a reflection of his heart toward God.

Abel did just the opposite. He had a reverent fear of God. He brought to God, not only the right offering, but a faithful and obedient heart, according to what a holy God had required. This is why God had regard for Abel and his offering. The word *regard* in these verses means "respect." God looked upon Abel and his offering with respect. He looked upon Cain and his offering with no respect.

We are told in Genesis 4:16 that Cain went out from the presence of the Lord. Sin and disobedience will always hinder or thwart intimacy with God.

> Then Moses said to Aaron, "It is what the Lord spoke, saying, 'By those who come near Me I will be treated as holy, and before all the people I will be honored.'" So Aaron, therefore, kept silent. Leviticus 10:3

Throughout the book of Leviticus God sets in order the rules of holiness and sacrifice. He tells Moses exactly what to sacrifice, how to sacrifice it, and when. God was making for Himself a holy people that they might know intimacy with God.

God is holy and if we are to be close to Him, we will treat Him as holy. We will have regard for Him and His Word. We will make the sacrifices that are necessary for our coming to Him.

God is holy. He desires to be treated as holy by all who come near to Him.

Are you beginning to see how sacrificial obedience leads to intimacy with God?

And what about Abraham? He was asked by God to make the sacrifice of all sacrifices. God asked Abraham to offer up Isaac, his only son, whom he loved.

Not only was Abraham *willing to be made willing*, but he was faithfully obedient to what God had asked of him. We will look at Abraham's life in depth a little later in this book.

PORTRAIT OF SACRIFICE

In the New Testament, Jesus Christ is the final blood sacrifice required by God for us to know intimacy with Him. This being so, is there a sacrifice that we are to make in order that we might know intimacy with God?

> Therefore I urge you, brethren, by the mercies of God, to present your bodies a living and holy sacrifice, acceptable to God, which is your spiritual service of worship. And do not be conformed to this world, but be transformed by the renewing of your mind, so that you may prove what the will of God is, that which is good and acceptable and perfect. Romans 12:1–2

There it is. The sacrifice that we are to make is the presentation of our total being as living, holy, and acceptable to God. Let's look together at a few more words to get a clearer portrait of sacrifice.

Present: The word *present* means to place beside for the purpose of making ready. I like that definition.

Bodies: The word *body* implies the total self—physical, spiritual, and emotional. Hold nothing back; give your all to God. Align yourself with Him and make your total self ready for His purpose.

Living: The word *living* means alive, quickened, active, and alert. It can also mean full of vigor, fresh, strong, and efficient.

Holy: A *holy* sacrifice is one that is pure, morally blameless, set apart for divine purposes.

Acceptable: The word *acceptable* means fully agreeable, well-pleasing. We really can stop here for a moment and examine our hearts. Many times we are so full of our own selves and our own schedules and agendas that the sacrifice of ourselves to God comes short of being acceptable. We must be fully agreeable with Him and what is well-pleasing to Him.

Let me commend those of you who are allowing God to work in this area of your life. As I travel, I can see women structuring their events and programs but also making room in their agendas for God to be God. May He bless your acceptable spirit.

Reasonable or Spiritual: Many Bible translations interpret the Greek word *logikos* as "reasonable" or "spiritual." This word is where we get the term *logical.* Something that is logical is expected because of what has gone on before. Don't you just love that?

Think about that definition as you look back at the way Paul began these two verses. *In view of God's mercies,* or because of what has gone on before. Paul thoroughly explained this in the first eleven chapters of Romans. He said making the daily sacrifice of your total self to God is just the *logical* thing to do.

Spiritually, it means the reasoning of the soul, or spiritually righteous. The sacrifice, or giving of ourselves to God for His purposes and not our own, is the spiritually righteous thing to do. Oh, this is getting good!

Conformed: The word *conformed* here means pressed into the mold. Don't let the world or unrighteousness press you into its mold. You have a different and higher calling in your life: you are set apart for God's purposes, not the purposes of the world or even your own.

Transformed: Changed! There is the hallmark of the Christian life. Change! The Greek word here is *metamorphoo*, from which we get the word *metamorphosis*. Metamorphosis is a change in form, structure, or function. It is the physical change that is undergone by certain animals, like a caterpillar to a butterfly. *Metamorphoo* is any *marked* change in character, appearance, or condition.

The words *conform* and *transform* are present imperative active in form. That means they are commands that are to be done now and in the future and are to involve continuous or repeated action. Therefore, we are to continually stop being conformed to the world and we are to continually be transformed by the renewing of our minds.

This change becomes a lifestyle, a daily presenting of your body or your total being to God.

Renewing: Hang on. *To renew* is to make new again. Old things will pass away and all things will become new again (2 Cor. 5:17). It means to renovate. A renewing is a complete change for the better!

Let there be a marked change in your life and character by the changing of your thoughts and motives for the better and the divine. Renewing the mind comes from looking into God's words and coming into total agreement with Him.

Prove: To *prove* means to test, to examine, and find to be true or false, genuine or not.

Will: God's *will* is His choice or His desire or pleasure.

Paul said to go on and make the sacrifice of yourself to God. Get face-to-face with Him. Let His Word change your thoughts and your character. By doing this you will find that His Word is true. His choice, desire, and pleasure are genuine. God encourages us to prove the authenticity of His will.

This brings intimacy. Can you see it? When you know someone, when you have allowed that person to influence you for the better and you find that their way is far better than your way, then you find intimacy. And you want it more and more.

Good: You may say, "Alicia, I don't need you to define the word *good*. I know what good means."

Great! But I am going to give you a few more words that will strengthen its meaning for you. The word *good* means beneficial, consisting of a pure nature, having the proper qualities, real, valid, virtuous, devout, thorough, useful, pleasant, agreeable, joyful, happy, excellent, distinguished, upright, honorable.

I get excited over the fact that God's will is agreeable. His will is not going to be something that I will not be able to come to grips with. Even when the diagnosis is cancer, if it is the will of God, it is agreeable, because His will is good. God's goodness means that there is no evil existing in Him.

> When the trumpeters and the singers were to make themselves heard with one voice to praise and to glorify the LORD, and when they lifted up their voice accompanied by trumpets and cymbals and instruments of music, and when they praised the LORD saying "*He indeed is good* for His lovingkindness is everlasting," then the house, the house of the LORD, was filled with a cloud, so that the priests could not stand to minister because of the cloud, for the glory of the LORD filled the house of God. 2 Chronicles 5:13–14

This passage tells of one of the rare occasions of corporate intimacy. I hope you are experiencing this kind of intimacy in your family of faith where you assemble yourselves for the purposes of God. First John 5:3 says that God's commands, or His will, are not burdensome. "And we know that God causes all things to work together for *good* to those who love God, to those who are called according to His *purpose*" (Rom. 8:28).

I will say it again. God causes, God allows, God is always in control! Glory to His holy name. God is good and His will is good.

Perfect: God's will is *perfect*. Perfect means finished! God is not in heaven wondering what He should do next. His will is finished. His will is not going to change. He reveals His will to us through His Word.

Now let me ask you: if you want to know intimacy with God, what do you think you should do? Meditate on Romans 12:1–2. Understand the words and their meaning, then write the verses so that you understand them completely. In doing this little exercise, you will begin to experience intimacy with God.

Present yourself as one who is dead to her own self-will and alive to the will of God. Come to Him daily and give your total self to Him, *holding nothing back.* Commit yourself to do the things that please God. This is where it all begins. Nothing counts for God until you begin here. This is your spiritual service of worship.

Know for certain that there is no getting around it. The obedient sacrificial presentation of our total selves is the first step on our journey toward intimacy with God, and this is what God-worshipers long for.

So what about you? What are you going to do with what you have just read? What is that you hold in your hand, in your head, and in your heart? How do you define your total self? Corrie Ten Boom once said she learned to hold *all things* loosely so that God would not have to pry them out of her hands. What great wisdom and insight!

Are you holding on to a husband or boyfriend or a relationship that brings you life and security? Are your children your treasure? I know how wonderful it is to be a mom, but my children belong to the Lord. I just get the honor and pleasure of being their mom for a little while.

Is your home where your heart is? Is your identity in the beauty or size of your house? We can honor God through how we take care of the beautiful home God gave us. Nevertheless, our identity is not to be in our homes that are here today and could be gone tomorrow.

The apostle Paul was a man who desired intimacy with God above all. He knew that the way to a deep personal relationship with Him was through the loss of all things, counting them as rubbish, that he might gain Christ (Phil. 3:7–14).

Are you willing? Are you *willing to be made willing*? If you are at least willing to be made willing then you are headed in the right direction toward a deeper intimacy with the One who loves you the most.

Hold nothing back! Let your life of obedient sacrifice lead you to intimacy with God. Yes, yes, Lord! Amen!

Chapter Two

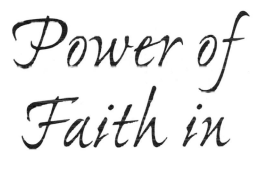

Power of Faith in Sacrifice

At the beginning of every year I try to set aside several days for prayer and fasting. I want to make sure I thank God for the year that has just passed, and I want to get clear direction from Him for the year to come. Sometimes I fast from food and sometimes from activities that just fill the day. My favorite days are when I am home alone with the televisions and telephones turned off, or when it's nice outside and I spend the day walking and talking with the Lord. At all costs I try to avoid all shopping, even for groceries, because this is a major distraction for me.

I start planning for my January prayer time in December. I get my January calendar out and plan about seven to ten days that I call "Praise the Lord Days." I try to set aside several hours each day just to have intimate time with God.

During the year I try to set aside one day a week as a "Praise the Lord Day." I try very hard to keep my mind on God's goodness. I praise Him all day long. I must admit that there are days when this is very difficult. But for me, good gospel music is all I need to keep me going.

I live near the Gulf of Mexico, so it is fun to ride on the bridges near the water with my CD-player blasting. Sometimes I sing along, sometimes I am crying so hard I can hardly see to drive. Praise the Lord Days are always spiritual breakthrough days for me.

If I am at home, I find myself dancing through the house or falling to my knees just to separate myself from the cares of the world and thank God for being God. You should try this sometime. There is power in praise!

These times of praise and thanksgiving go on and on, because there is so much to praise and thank God for. The more I thank Him, the more He shows me that there is even more to be thankful for. And the more I praise Him, the more He shows me that there is more to praise Him for.

I must tell you, God is always faithful to bless me with His powerful presence and speak to my heart as only He can. I look forward to these times every year and I try to make them special and eventful. One request I always make at the beginning of each year is that God would show me how to be a better wife. I ask him to show me how I can be my husband's best friend and greatest encouragement in all the different roles that he plays. Let me tell you, if you ask God to show you this, He will. Just prepare yourself to be the living sacrifice we talked about in chapter one.

Know also that the reward is greater than the sacrifice. Go on and do whatever God tells you. Be your husband's best friend (after all, he would rather you kiss him than his dog) and give him a reason to hurry home after work.

UNEDITED PRAYERS

The best prayer I can pray is an honest, unedited prayer. I remember one year praying (or, should I say, complaining) that my life was in a major rut. I just could not seem to get ahead. I kept slipping and sliding in the same ole mud. I hated admitting it, but it was true. I found myself pouring my heart out to God about it: "Lord, I want to be an over-comer this year! I don't want to get stuck in the same traps and spin my wheels in the same mud. I want to victoriously move forward! I've asked You, God, to show me how to be truly victorious in every area of my life, especially in the places that seem to never advance! You always answer me from Your Word. Please show me now."

I want you to know that God answered this prayer with one verse that had many of the same words I just prayed. That moment with God was mighty powerful. He really does speak to us through His Word.

God gave me this word from the book of Joshua: "This book of the law shall not depart from your mouth, but you shall meditate on it day and night, so that you may be careful to do according to all that is written in it; for then you will make your way prosperous, and then you will have success" (Josh. 1:8).

Pretty direct answer, wouldn't you say? Now let me take you through the little exercise that I then did. It got even more exciting. Because I was so desperate to advance in life, the first thing I did was make a list of everything this verse told me to do.

1. This book of the law shall not depart from your mouth.
2. You shall meditate on it day and night.
3. (so that) You may be careful to do according to all that is written in it.
4. (for) Then you will make your way prosperous.
5. (and then) You will have success.

I reviewed the list to make sure I understood every word. Here is what I found.

1. This book of the law is the Word of God, and I am to keep His Word, not my doubts and fears, in my mouth.

How will I do that?

2. I shall meditate on it, the Word of God. When? Day and night!

What does it mean to meditate? To *meditate* means to think deeply, to mutter, to muse. The words *mutter* and *muse* are very close in meaning: to speak slowly in distinct tones.

Oh I get it. I need to read God's words aloud, slowly, with the purpose of understanding them and not just getting through them with a surface knowledge. I need to slow down and think deeply about what God is saying. This will take the sacrifice of time and a little research. It will also take disciplining myself to direct my focus on God's Word.

3. The Word of God is never to depart from my mouth.

I accomplish that by speaking God's Word out loud, with the purpose of understanding it. Why? So that I may be careful to do according to all that is written in it.

I immediately recognized the element of faith! There is something I must do. I am to get the Word of God in me, think about it day and night, speak it slowly so that I thoroughly understand it. And I am to be careful to do what it says.

Now that I understood that completely, I thought I would get theological with God. "But God, this is the Old Testament. I am under a New Covenant. What about grace?"

In my heart I heard God say, "Do you want to advance or not?"

As I thought about what He had just asked me, I knew He was saying that He was giving me the short version, and I needed to just trust what He was saying.

I got over the Old Testament questions quickly, and then kept going. I really wanted to advance in life.

4. For then you will make your way prosperous.

I will be honest. I really struggled with this, because I was feeling like such a failure. How could I possibly make my way prosperous? I questioned God again, but not with an arrogant heart. This time, I really sought to understand what He was saying. I wanted this so badly. He told me to read the verse again. I read it over and over and over. I must have read it twenty times, slowly, word for word. Then finally, I got it.

There were two key words in this phrase for me, *then* and *prosperous*. The word *then* meant after something else, and I needed to be sure I knew what the something else was.

The word *prosperous* did not mean at all what I first thought; and to tell you the truth, I am really glad. The word prosperous here is not about financial gain; it is about advancing in life. This was a direct answer from God to my prayer. I would not have known that if I had stopped with the understanding I had when I first read this verse. Now I was getting really excited.

The word prosperous means to advance, to make progress, to succeed, to be profitable, to push forward (literally or figuratively). I did not care how I had to push forward. As long as God's Word was telling me I could do it, I was willing to do whatever it took to get out of the rut I was in.

Prosperous also means to thrive, or flourish, or to grow robust.

Yes! This is what I wanted! According to this word, I had a responsibility toward my own prosperity. I know that Jesus said that without Him I can do nothing (John 15:5). But what was my responsibility in making my way prosperous? Once again I read the verse, slowly, with the purpose of understanding it. Finally the Holy Spirit revealed truth (John 16:13–15).

If I fully believed and received what God was saying in this verse, I would respond obediently to it. If His Word was therefore in my mouth day and night, it was probably going to be in my heart. If it was in my heart, then I was going to live differently and make different decisions. I would choose according to the Word of the Lord. These better choices would make me prosperous. I would be able to get out of the rut that I had been in for several years.

This was a direct answer to prayer.

5. God said that I would have success.

I dug a little deeper to make sure I understood what God was saying, and again the richness of His Word filled my heart. The entire phrase, "You will have success," is one word: *sakal.* It means prudence, wise understanding, intelligence. The result of this wisdom and intelligence is good success, prosperity, advancing, pushing ahead—exactly what I had asked God for.

Here again is my prayer. Read it slowly.

> "Lord, I want to be an overcomer this year! I don't want to get stuck in the same traps and spin my wheels in the same mud. I want to victoriously move forward! Please show me how to be truly victorious in every area of my life, especially in the places that seem to never advance."

Here is God's answer. Now that you understand it, read it slowly.

> This book of the law shall not depart from your mouth, but you shall meditate on it day and night, so that you may be careful to do according to all that is written in it; for then you will make your way prosperous, and then you will have success. Joshua 1:8

This direct answer to prayer even uses some of the same words I used. I knew God was speaking to me and I have come to love and trust the Bible. All I needed was His Word.

ANSWERED PRAYER

I got out of that rut and my life has not stopped advancing since. I am experiencing new and exciting things in ministry all the time. That was the area I had really prayed about. I did not want to be someone who had to ask for things in ministry. I wanted God's favor to rise up in the hearts of those who could help me. God did just that. Just a short time after I had prayed this prayer and started responding in faith to what God had told me, I got a letter in the mail asking me to write my first book. I was overjoyed. I did not know that New Hope Publishers even knew my name, and here they were asking me to write on my favorite subject, worship.

Shortly after that, I sang at a chapel service early one morning. I did not even want to be there, but I felt like God wanted me there. I obeyed and sang and shared my testimony. A man walked in and heard only the last ten minutes of the service, but called my husband afterward and said he felt like his company wanted to do a live praise and worship record with me.

This was exactly what I had been hoping to do. And I have to tell you, it felt great not to have to ask. He made the offer three times before I responded. I wanted to make sure this was God and not just my desire to do another record.

This same kind of thing happened when I was dealing with cancer. When I knew in my heart, because God had given me His Word, that God had a greater plan for me than cancer, I found that the cancer was completely gone. Then He surprised us with a baby boy, Michael Chandler. If that were not enough, we now have another son, Richard David. God is good!

Jesus says that if we abide in Him and His words abide in us, we can ask whatever we wish, and it will be done for us (John 15:7). Sounds a little like "name it, claim it," but it is not at all. Three times in His most intimate teachings to His closest friends, Jesus gave the disciples the prerequisite for answered prayer, and that is to ask in His name, or His character, or His nature. Ask like Jesus would ask, according to the Word of God, which is the will of God.

Why is this important? Because intimacy with God will bring about a heart that is cultivated toward the will and desire of God. Our prayers are then prayed, even unedited, within the will of God. These God-willed prayers are the ones Jesus says are always answered.

To abide means to be at home with, to be comfortable with. My dear friend Cynthia Heald says that to abide is to sit at Jesus' feet, listening to His words, with a heart to obey. She is exactly right, and it does not get any more clearly stated than that.

The book of the law will not depart from us, day or night, because we have learned to abide in Christ. We have His Word abiding in us. Jesus promises that abiding in His Word not only brings about answered prayer but also intimacy with God (John 14:21, 23, 16:13).

God's Word also teaches us that the prayer offered in faith, which also means according to the Word and will of God, will restore the one who is sick and the Lord will raise them up (James 5:15).

Therefore, answered prayer begins with abiding in the Word of God. The Word of God then brings about intimacy and friendship with God, as He discloses Himself to us. Our faith grows in the character of God and we begin to pray in His name, just like Jesus said.

So what about you? Are you ready to advance? Are you tired of spinning your wheels in the same old mud? Is it time for you to move ahead? Be encouraged, I have great news for you!

Progress and prosperity come as a result of meditating on the Word of God, abiding in His Word, and letting His Word be at home in you. Advancement comes when we receive God's truth in our hearts and are careful to do according to all that is written in it.

If we say we believe the word of God, then that faith should be evidenced in the way we live. Our faithful response will always bring about intimacy with our holy God. How wonderful! How marvelous!

God does not operate in an atmosphere of fear. He operates in the atmosphere of faith, the faith that comes from knowing God's Word.

Why did I take you through all of this? To show you how intimate and honest and real our prayer time can be when we exercise faith in God and His Word. These are but a few of the many miracles I have seen in my own life. They have come because I chose to believe God's Word!

FAITH DEFINED

So just what is faith? The Bible says that the righteous shall live by faith (Rom. 1:17). We have no options. If we are going to live lives that please God, then we must live by faith.

The Bible tells us that faith comes by hearing the Word of Christ (Rom. 10:17). Faith is not something we can bottle up and give away. It comes only when we hear the Word of Christ. Whenever we want to encourage someone in the faith, it is important to share the Word of God with him or her. Stories motivate and can encourage, but the Word of God within the story is what will change a life.

The Bible also says that without faith, it is impossible to please God (Heb. 11:6). Here again we are left with no options. If we choose an option in life that is contrary to the faith that comes from God's Word, then our lives are not pleasing to God.

Hebrews 11:1 is that great Bible verse that introduces God's Hall of Faith and gives us the definition of faith:

> Now faith is the assurance of things hoped for, the conviction of things not seen.

Let's spend a little time with this verse, just so that we know we understand it.

Faith: Of course, we could get into a big discussion on the full meaning of faith, but for this book, we only need to know that faith is belief. Spiritually, it is moral conviction.

Assurance: Assurance is substance! Webster's dictionary says that substance is the real or essential part of anything. It is the physical matter of which a thing consists. Substance is solid, of substantial quality, the real meaning or gist.

Hope: Hope is joyful, confident expectation. This is exactly what I received when I was sick with cancer and the Lord Jesus came to me with the Word of God. That Word produced faith, which is comprised of this joyful, confident hope! Hang on!

Evidence: We all know what evidence is. Certainly you have seen enough courtroom television to know what this word means. Evidence is proof. Spiritually, evidence goes deeper than just the hard-core facts. Spiritually, evidence is conviction, heart-felt proof that comes from the Word of God.

Are you beginning to see how essential the Word of God is to our faith? Then you should begin to understand that whatever sacrifices God requires of us must be sacrifices of faith. We do what we do because we believe what we believe. We believe because we have seen the truth of God's Word. Without faith, the sacrifice will not please God (Heb. 11:6). Faith comes from trusting, knowing, and believing God's Word (Rom. 10:17). The righteous shall live by faith (Rom. 1:17). We have no options.

THE RESPONSIBILITY OF FAITH

Faith is more than the mental or heart-felt reception of truth. It is the acting out of that truth.

Biblical belief, or faith, always demands a response! We cannot say we believe and then not respond or do something. Faith always demands a response!

We are going to talk about obedience in the next chapter, and that will bring to full circle this discussion on faith. Just know for now that you cannot say you believe one thing and live another. We all have faith. We all live what we believe.

For example, I believe that brushing my teeth is important, so I do that daily. I believe in good hygiene, so I do that every day. I believe hugs and kisses for my family are very important, so I do that every single day. I do not believe that dinner is all that important, so I don't always do that!

For certain, we live what we believe. Make a list of everything you do on a daily basis; you will see your faith. You may find that you need to make some adjustments or sacrifices so that your life is aligned with God's Word.

I believe the Bible, so I strive to live according to God's Word daily. I believe in the power of prayer, so I pray daily. I believe in praise and thanksgiving and repentance, so as best I can, I do these things daily.

You may be saying, "Alicia, Alicia, ease up! Christianity is not about what we do, it is about what Christ has done." Yes, this is totally true! Nevertheless, if we say that we believe what Christ has done, if we say we believe in the finished work of Jesus Christ, then we will have changed lives, and that change will be reflected in what we do or how we live.

POWER OF FAITH

I mentioned earlier that we are going to take a close look at the life of Abraham later on, but it is hard not to say a word about him now, since we refer to him as the father of our faith, and for all the right reasons.

In Genesis 22:2 we learn that Abraham was asked to sacrifice his son. God was very specific about this sacrifice.

> Take now your son, your only son, whom you love, Isaac, and go to the land of Moriah, and offer him there as a burnt offering on one of the mountains of which I will tell you.

God told Abraham, "Take the son whom you love," and called him by his name, Isaac. While the concept of love is mentioned earlier in Genesis, this is the first time the word *love* is mentioned in all of the Word of God.

Abraham knew that he was to offer Isaac, whom he loved deeply, as a burnt offering. Abraham was a man of worship and he understood what it meant to bring sacrifices and burnt offerings. (We will see that more clearly later on.) In this story, Abraham knew that he was to offer Isaac on an altar of fire, and that his precious son was to be totally consumed. Abraham was to hold nothing back!

A burnt offering was also classified as a voluntary offering or a love offering, indicating that Abraham had a choice. Yet we see in verse 3 that without hesitation, Abraham readied himself and Isaac to do what God had asked of him.

> So Abraham rose early in the morning and saddled his donkey, and took two of his young men with him and Isaac his son; and he split wood for the burnt offering, and arose and went to the place of which God had told him. . . . Then they came to the place of which God had told him; and Abraham built the altar there and arranged the wood, and bound his son Isaac and laid him on the altar, on top of the wood. Abraham stretched out his hand and took the knife to slay his son. Genesis 22:3, 9–10

Where did Abraham get the power or the strength to exercise this kind of faith? What was it that fueled his fire and got him going? Let's look into the heart of Abraham and see if we can find some answers there.

Here is the only recorded conversation between Abraham and Isaac during the three-day trip to Moriah. Abraham's intentions were obvious to all, so Isaac's question was valid. Take special note of Abraham's answer.

> Isaac spoke to Abraham his father and said, "My father!" And he said, "Here I am, my son." And he said, "Behold, the fire and the wood, but where is the lamb for the burnt offering?" Abraham said, "God will provide for Himself the lamb for the burnt offering, my son." So the two of them walked on together. Genesis 22:7–8

Now let's look at some biblical commentary on this event from the book of Hebrews.

> By faith Abraham, when he was tested, offered up Isaac, and he who had received the promises was offering up his only begotten son; it was he to whom it was said, "IN ISAAC

> YOUR DESCENDANTS SHALL BE CALLED." He [Abraham]
> considered that God is able to raise people even from the
> dead, from which he also received him back as a type.
> Hebrews 11:17–19

In Genesis 22 God gave Abraham a direct command. In the very next verse Abraham responded without hesitation. In verses 7 and 8, Abraham carried out God's command. Hebrews 11:17–18 helps us understand what Abraham believed.

Abraham believed in the faithful character of God. By this time in his life, he had followed God for years and had seen God's faithfulness even when he had made terrible mistakes.

Abraham knew that God was merciful and forgiving. Abraham had faith in God, knowing He was a redeemer and that He could make good out of a bad situation. Abraham knew, beyond a doubt, that God was faithful. Because of God's unblemished character, Abraham believed that God would fulfill His promise in the life or death of his precious Isaac.

The power in Abraham's life to make the sacrifice of sacrifices came from his full faith in God. The power of sacrifice in your life and mine will come from knowing the Word of God. Our responsibility then is to study the Word so it will dwell richly in our hearts, strengthen our faith, and change our lives for the glory and honor of Almighty God.

It takes faith to sacrifice, faith to let it all go. But once again the reward is greater than the sacrifice. The end of verse 19 says that Abraham received back his Isaac from the dead, and Isaac has become for us a picture of what we are to be to God: living sacrifices.

We will take an even closer look at Abraham's faith and obedience in the next chapter.

INTIMATE FAITH

Abraham was a man of faith, a worshiper, a man of sacrifice, but never had God called him to give up the one thing that held eternal promise for him. Searching his heart, Abraham saw great love for Isaac and a deep desire to inherit all of God's promises. But greater than all of these, he found in his heart the greatest love of all, a deep, intimate, and perfect love for God.

> There is no fear in love; but perfect love casts out fear, because fear involves punishment, and the one who fears is not perfected in love. 1 John 4:18

Fear is the opposite of faith. Abraham did have a reverent fear of a holy God, which is what God's Word teaches us to have. Faith is the only thing that dispels fear. During his most crucial hour, Abraham's love for God was put to the test, but He was able to say, like I hope you and I can, that he loved God more than any other precious person or thing in his life. Because of this, His faith grew strong and His experience with God more intimate. This experience created for Abraham intimacy with God that comes only through abiding faith.

———❦———

Chapter Three

Proper Obedience in Sacrifice

———❦———

J am one who would rather ask forgiveness than permission. It seems easier to get forgiveness, so I just go on and do what I want to do, without permission, and if I offend someone, he or she will just have to forgive me. That's terrible, but I must admit, that is the route I sometimes take. I wonder if any of you are like me. This behavior is not a good thing, so I hope that you are better than I am.

Unfortunately, I do this with my beloved Richard. He is so patient with me. Often I will buy something that I think we need, but that he thinks we can wait on. My philosophy is, "Why wait?" Tomorrow is not promised, and if it will bring glory to God or lots of fun to our lives today, then why not?

So far so good! My little philosophy has worked and I have always gotten forgiveness, but that is because my husband is such a wonderful man. Nevertheless, my heart is becoming more tender, and I know I need to honor him and not be crafty with him. (I do know what the Bible says about craftiness, so you don't have to send me letters.) My heart needs to change because this type of attitude affects my obedience to God.

I commend you for reading up to this point, and I hope the subject of sacrificial living is beginning to sink in. Christianity is all about sacrificial living. Everything we do, if we are living like true worshipers of Jesus Christ, will have the element of sacrifice in it.

Writing this book, as fun and exciting as it is, is a major sacrifice for me. The only time I get to write is in the early morning. Every day when I get out of bed I say to God, "This feels like a sacrifice." I can always hear His gentle whisper in my heart, "Yes! It is that indeed. Without a sacrifice, there is no worship."

I want to be a true worshiper, and worship always involves the element of sacrifice. Your reading this book and allowing God's truth to penetrate your heart and change your life involves the sacrifice of your own time and self-will, that you might know and do the will of God.

Quiet time with God will have the element of sacrifice. Loving our husbands and children will have the element of sacrifice. Loving and serving others will have the element of sacrifice. Discipleship and the lifestyle of worship involve the giving up of ourselves for the advancement of the kingdom of God. We have already seen this in Romans 12:1–2. There is no way around it. The life we live, if it is to be pleasing to God, will be a life of sacrifice.

CHRIST'S OBEDIENCE

In Jesus Christ we see a life of obedient sacrifice. He lived to *do* the will of His Father. More than He wanted to make friends, He wanted to make disciples. Jesus said in John 5:30, "I can do nothing on My own initiative. As I hear, I judge; and My judgment is just, because I do not seek My own will, but the will of Him who sent Me."

The writer of Hebrews said of Jesus, "Although He was a Son, He learned obedience from the things which He suffered (Heb. 5:8).

Jesus learned obedience through the things that He suffered! Jesus Christ is the Son of God who became the Son of Man. As the Son of God, He knew no disobedience. He and the Father are one. Their will is one and the same. There was no disobedience. But as the Son of Man, there was within Him a free will. He had the choice of His will or the will of the Father.

Remember Jesus' prayer in the Garden of Gethsemane just before He was arrested? "Abba! Father! All things are possible for You; remove this cup from Me; yet not what *I will*, but what *You will*" (Mark 14:36). He had a choice and He chose the will of the Father.

This was not just a one-time decision. We know that all through His life, Jesus was tempted, as we are, with all sin, but never once did He yield to sin (Heb. 4:15). He chose the will of His Father over the will of His flesh. He learned obedience through the things He suffered all through His life as the incarnate Son of God, even through the sacrificial, obedient suffering of the cross.

What did Jesus gain as a result of His sacrificial obedience to the Father?

> And having been made perfect, He became to all those who obey Him the source of eternal salvation, being designated by God as a high priest according to the order of Melchizedek. Hebrews 5:9–10

Having been made perfect—living out through sacrificial obedience what He knew and believed about the Father—Jesus became the source of eternal salvation. He is designated or appointed by God as the eternal high priest, or advocate, or mediator between God and mankind.

Now Jesus is the eternal high priest for all those who obey Him. And there it is. Access to God is, of course, through Christ. Not for those who just say they belong to Christ, but for those who obey Him. That is not Alicia; that is the Bible. Read the verse again if you need to.

How we live, the motive behind all of our intentions, and what we *do*, really does matter. The hallmark of true Christianity is obedience. The key to understanding the Christian life is to understand that the lessons and disciplines that we learn along our journey are not only one-time events, but they are to become our obedient, sacrificial way of life.

INCOMPLETE OBEDIENCE IS DISOBEDIENCE

The Israelites learned this lesson the hard way. God, through His servant Joshua, had given the Israelites specific instructions for taking the land that He had promised them. They were told to go in and destroy everyone, all their idols, and to get rid of all their stuff. The Israelites did this partially. They destroyed lots of people, idols, and stuff, but left for themselves all that they thought would give glory to God or enjoyment to themselves and their families. They were obedient, but their obedience was incomplete.

In the book of Judges, we see the results of the Israelites' actions and the pattern set up by their disobedience. God judged the people, and they cried out to God. God raised up a judge to lead the people. He provided the people with victory and helped them through that judge. But when the judge died, the people sinned, and God brought judgment upon them again. They would cry out to God again, and God would raise up another judge, and there would be the help of God's presence until that judge died.

This cycle of judges, sin, and judgment lasted for more than 300 years, until finally their apathy toward God turned to apostasy, and apostasy led to anarchy. The book of Judges closes with a very sad, key, repeated phrase: "In those days there was no king in Israel; everyone did what was right in his own eyes" (Judges 21:25).

If we are apathetic in our obedience toward God, then apathy will lead us to apostasy, which means turning away. We will begin to think that we can compromise God's

Word and His commands, or abuse (but never exhaust) His grace. We drift away from absolute truth and become king or queen of our own lives. There is no living to please God, no presenting ourselves as living sacrifices. We live to please ourselves, doing what is right in our own eyes. How dangerous. How very dangerous.

After the period of judges, God appointed Saul to be Israel's king. Saul was a fine king of Israel until he, too, chose incomplete rather than sacrificial obedience to God. Saul was instructed by God to do one thing, but he thought it best to do another. He thought his idea was better than God's and that God would change His mind and agree that Saul's decision was the better one for Israel. Saul was sadly mistaken.

God says what He means and means what He says. He speaks the truth, and there is only one proper response: sacrificial, full, and immediate obedience.

Let's look for a moment at 1 Samuel 15.

> Then Samuel said to Saul, "The LORD sent me to anoint you as king over His people, over Israel; now therefore, listen to the words of the LORD." 1 Samuel 15:1

Now that's the key! Listen to the words of the Lord! Oh, the mistakes and hindrances we would avoid if we would, with all of our hearts, listen to the words of the Lord. Perhaps already you are reading through these verses too fast. Slow down! This is not a speed-reading course. Let the words of God penetrate your heart and change your life. Though we are reading the story of someone else, we can benefit from the lessons. Listen to the words of the Lord!

> "Thus says the LORD of hosts, 'I will punish Amalek for what he did to Israel, how he set himself against him on

the way while he was coming up from Egypt. Now go and strike Amalek and utterly destroy all that he has, and do not spare him; but put to death both man and woman, child and infant, ox and sheep, camel and donkey.'" 1 Samuel 15:2–3

Whose job was it to destroy Amalek? How was he going to do it? What were God's specific instructions to Saul? Read on and follow carefully the words of the Lord and Saul's response.

Then Saul summoned the people and numbered them in Telaim, 200,000 foot soldiers and 10,000 men of Judah. Saul came to the city of Amalek and set an ambush in the valley. Saul said to the Kenites, "Go, depart, go down from among the Amalekites, so that I do not destroy you with them; for you showed kindness to all the sons of Israel when they came up from Egypt." So the Kenites departed from among the Amalekites. So Saul defeated the Amalekites, from Havilah as you go to Shur, which is east of Egypt. 1 Samuel 15:4–7

So far so good, but Saul's big mistake of compromise comes in the following verses. God had said destroy *all* that Amalek had. Saul thought he had a better idea.

He captured Agag the king of the Amalekites alive, and utterly destroyed all the people with the edge of the sword. But Saul and the people spared Agag and the best of the sheep, the oxen, the fatlings, the lambs, and all that was good, and were not willing to destroy them utterly; but everything despised and worthless, that they utterly destroyed. 1 Samuel 15:8–9

Perhaps Saul and the people thought they would do God a favor and spare Agag, King of Amalek, and all the good stuff. This could perhaps bring glory to God or good to the people. Nevertheless, it was not what God had told them to do. This is another classic example of incomplete obedience, which is disobedience.

OBEDIENCE GREATER THAN SACRIFICE

The things that Saul spared are a picture of the flesh and that which is temporal. These things will never sufficiently substitute for the eternal gifts of God, which come through sacrificial obedience. Let's look now at God's response and judgment upon Saul's disobedience.

> Then the word of the LORD came to Samuel, saying, "I regret that I have made Saul king, for he has turned back from following Me and has not carried out My commands." And Samuel was distressed and cried out to the LORD all night. 1 Samuel 15:10–11

The things that break God's heart should also break ours. His concerns are to be our concerns. He cares that His children are obedient to His word because He knows the benefits of obedience. We are to simply trust that God really does know what is best for us. Samuel's heart broke over the disobedience of a fellow servant, and he cried out to God all night in intercession. He prayed to have God's words for his fellow servant who had failed to follow God's commands.

> Samuel rose early in the morning to meet Saul; and it was told Samuel, saying, "Saul came to Carmel, and behold, he set up a monument for himself, then turned and proceeded on down to Gilgal." Samuel came to Saul, and Saul said to him, "Blessed are you of the LORD! I have carried out the command of the LORD." 1 Samuel 15:12–13

Saul said one thing but God said another. Look at the contrast.

> But Samuel said, "What then is this bleating of the sheep in my ears, and the lowing of the oxen which I hear?" Saul said, "They have brought them from the Amalekites, for the people spared the best of the sheep and oxen, to sacrifice to the LORD your God; but the rest we have utterly destroyed." 1 Samuel 15:14–15

Saul thought he had a better idea than God's perfect command. He saved what he thought were the better parts, that he might sacrifice them to God. Sounds like a godly idea to me. *Godly* means "like God." Yet, when what we do does not totally line up with what God has commanded us to do, then regardless of how pretty and godly our doing may look, it is still less than perfect. It is still not like God! My suggestion is that you hold nothing back, but let sacrificial obedience lead to intimacy with God or suffer the consequences. Let's keep going.

> Then Samuel said to Saul, "Wait, and let me tell you what the LORD said to me last night." And he said to him, "Speak!" Samuel said, "Is it not true, though you were little in your own eyes, you were made the head of the tribes of Israel? And the LORD anointed you king over Israel, and the LORD sent you on a mission, and said, 'Go and utterly destroy the sinners, the Amalekites, and fight against them until they are exterminated.' Why then did you not obey the voice of the LORD, but rushed upon the spoil and did what was evil in the sight of the LORD?" 1 Samuel 15:16–19

Watch how Saul tried to get around the question.

> Then Saul said to Samuel, "I did obey the voice of the LORD, and went on the mission on which the LORD sent me, and have brought back Agag the king of Amalek, and have utterly destroyed the Amalekites." 1 Samuel 15:20

Saul's idea of obedience was obviously different from God's idea of obedience. He brought others into his disobedience and still tried to make their doing look like a noble act of love toward God. If God says we have disobeyed, then we need to acknowledge that we have disobeyed. Saul continued to make excuses.

> "But the people took some of the spoil, sheep and oxen, the choicest of the things devoted to destruction, to sacrifice to the LORD your God at Gilgal." 1 Samuel 15:21

Here now is the lesson that we all must learn once and for all. Samuel's words to Saul and to us are directly from the heart of a holy and just God.

> Samuel said, "Has the LORD as much delight in burnt offerings and sacrifices as in obeying the voice of the LORD? Behold, to obey is better than sacrifice, and to heed than the fat of rams." 1 Samuel 15:22

God delights in our obedience more than our sacrifice. Living in obedience shows that we love God and that we trust His words. We have already seen that we are to live by faith, and that there is no other option if we are to please God. We have also seen that without trust in God's words, we fail in our attempts to please God.

What we call sacrifices can very easily be gestures that save our own face or bring glory to others, having only a pretense of bringing glory to God. Let's make sure that we sacrifice according to the will of God and not according to our own will and agenda.

Does the Lord delight more in our sacrifices and offerings than He does in our obedience to Him? No! To obey is better than sacrifice!

TORN FROM INTIMACY

Samuel described Saul's sin to him and showed him how devastating it was to reject the words of the Lord. Saul confessed his sin and asked for forgiveness, but God had already announced judgment. Repentance must come before judgment.

> "For rebellion is as the sin of divination, and insubordination is as iniquity and idolatry. Because you have rejected the word of the LORD, He has also rejected you from being king." Then Saul said to Samuel, "I have sinned; I have indeed transgressed the command of the LORD and your words, because I feared the people and listened to their voice. Now therefore, please pardon my sin and return with me, that I may worship the LORD." But Samuel said to Saul, "I will not return with you; for you have rejected the word of the LORD, and the LORD has rejected you from being king over Israel." As Samuel turned to go, Saul seized the edge of his robe, and it tore. So Samuel said to him, "The LORD has torn the kingdom of Israel from you today and has given it to your neighbor, who is better than you. Also the Glory of Israel will not lie or change His mind; for He is not a man that He should change His mind." 1 Samuel 15:23–29

God is not a man that He should lie, or a son of man that He should change His mind (Num. 23:19). His Word, His purposes are forever settled in the heavens (Psalm 119:89). His Word comes to us that we might escape His wrath. Obedience is not a suggestion but a command. God is holy, and all those who worship or approach Him must treat Him as holy (Lev. 10:3).

BUT THE PEOPLE . . .

Did you notice that Saul used the people as an excuse for his disobedience? Blaming someone else is very popular, it seems. God has been hearing this excuse since Adam blamed Eve and the serpent for his disobedience.

Saul was king, but he was separating his actions from those of the people. He was wrong to do that! The people were under his command, and God had already told him to destroy everything belonging to Amalek. If the people were to join him in obeying God, then they were to follow the same commands that God had given Saul, and Saul's responsibility was to see that God's commands were carried out in his kingdom.

Saul then told Samuel that he did obey God but that the people were disobedient. He tried to divert Samuel's attention from himself onto the people. But Samuel was not moved by Saul's excuses. Saul had sinned and God appointed Samuel to pronounce judgment. Verse 24 really says it all:

> Then Saul said to Samuel, "I have sinned; I have indeed transgressed the command of the LORD and your words, because I feared the people and listened to their voice."

Saul feared the people and listened to them. He did not listen to the Lord's command. The lesson is very simple: we are to fear God and not man. God is the One who will judge our deeds; therefore, we are to be careful to do all that God commands. He will not accept excuses; He will only judge our response to His commands (2 Cor. 5:10).

SAVE MY FACE

How did this story end? As you can imagine, the ending was a sad one for King Saul. He asked Samuel to save his face before the elders of Israel, that he might worship the Lord again. Samuel did go back home with Saul. Saul worshiped the Lord, but Samuel did not participate in this worship service. Instead, Samuel killed Agag and carried out the command of the Lord. Samuel departed and did not bring the words of the Lord to Saul ever again.

> Then he said, "I have sinned; but please honor me now before the elders of my people and before Israel, and go back with me, that I may worship the LORD your God." So Samuel went back following Saul, and Saul worshiped the LORD. Then Samuel said, "Bring me Agag, the king of the Amalekites." And Agag came to him cheerfully. And Agag said, "Surely the bitterness of death is past." But Samuel said, "As your sword has made women childless, so shall your mother be childless among women." And Samuel hewed Agag to pieces before the LORD at Gilgal. Then Samuel went to Ramah, but Saul went up to his house at Gibeah of Saul. Samuel did not see Saul again until the day of his death; for Samuel grieved over Saul. And the LORD regretted that He had made Saul king over Israel. 1 Samuel 15:30–35

Obedience is big time with God. He wants our obedience, which is based on faith in Him! I pray that you and I will never give God reason to regret the grace that He has shown us. If perhaps you do feel rejected, go to God with a humble heart. Confess your sin, and allow His holy Word to cleanse you again. God is a Redeemer, and if we seek His righteousness, Jesus said, we will find it (Matt. 5:6). God is holy and He desires to be treated as holy.

BUT HE DID REPENT

Yes, I know that in verses 24 and 30 it looks as if Saul repented and wanted to make things right between himself and God, but take a closer look and see what is really happening in these verses.

First be reminded of the definitions of *repent* and *confess*. To *repent* means to go in the opposite direction, and *to confess* our sin means to agree with God.

Saul did not agree with God that what he did was wrong. In verse 24 Saul's confession was laced with blame. He made excuses for his sin. This is not the mark of true confession. True confession says God is right and I am wrong. It does not add any condition. Repentance is a turning away from wrong and *turning to* that which is right. The turning to what is right is very important because we can easily turn from one wrong to another wrong. True repentance turns away from wrong and turns to "thus saith the Lord."

Saul had the old "the Devil made me do it" syndrome. Whereas this kind of confession will sometimes get us forgiveness with man, it will never wash with God. God is not a man that He should lie. God is true and His Word is true. He requires truth in our inmost being. God not only searches our words, He searches our hearts (Psalm 51).

When I was in college I had to memorize a phrase that has helped me ever since. I do not know the author of this little phrase, but it sure is a good one: "Excuses are the tools of the incompetent, and those who specialize in them are seldom capable of anything."

My mom is a retired public school teacher. She taught for thirty-one years, and she has heard every excuse in the book. I remember going home from college one weekend and wanting money for something. I tried to get the money from my mom, but when she questioned me about my need, I just made up a bunch of excuses why I was out of money and needed more. I will never forget her response. She said, "Excuses are lies. Reasons are truth." If I had had a legitimate reason for needing more money, she would have been glad to give it. She was not falling for my excuses, though. They really were lies. So what did I do? I did what every wise daughter does . . . I asked my dad!

But why didn't I just tell the truth? I needed mo' money because I spent what I had on what I wanted, and not on the purpose for which it was intended. I had sinned, nothing more. No excuses. The reason was, I sinned. Confession would have been good for my soul. I did the wrong thing and needed grace to make it right. Mom was trying to teach me a great lesson, but I was like Saul. I thought my excuses were good enough for me to get what I was seeking.

In verse 30, we do not see genuine repentance from Saul. Saul's affection was not for Samuel or for God. He was only interested in his own reputation before the elders. This is not repentance. Saul was not interested in doing the right thing; he was only interested in looking right before the people. Sounds like some politicians to me. It may be used often in politics, but it is bad theology.

Confession will always say that God is right and I am wrong, nothing added. Repentance will always turn to what is right, without regard for self.

THE OLD TESTAMENT

Why do we have to visit the Old Testament? If we are New Testament believers, then what is there in the Old Testament for us? *Everything*! It is very important to seek to understand the whole of Scripture and not to just study our favorite parts, or only the things we want to see or hear. As I have said earlier, we must seek to understand the whole counsel of God. The New Testament helps us understand the Old Testament more completely as it reveals and fulfills the teachings of the Old Testament. Let's look briefly at some Old Testament passages and listen carefully to God's heart on the subject of obedience.

If you have read *A Seeking Heart: Rediscovering True Worship* or if you have worked your way through the study guide, then you know many Old Testament stories about people who lost fellowship with God because of disobedience or a lack of regard for the words of God. You know that the subject of obedience in Scripture goes all the way back to Adam and Eve. We also learned a very big word, *perspicuous*. God is perspicuous. He means to be understood.

(If you have not read *A Seeking Heart*, then let me suggest that you do. You will want to get the study guide as well, because going through it will slow you down so that the Word of God really gets into your heart.)

We are not going to revisit those stories here; we are simply going to look at a few verses that will give us a good overview of the heart of God.

The first verses are from the book of Deuteronomy, where God gives mankind His Law. Have you ever wondered why God gave us the Law? The answer is very simple. God gave us the Law to teach us His righteousness.

> Therefore the Law has become our tutor to lead us to Christ, so that we may be justified by faith. Galatians 3:24

So the Law came to teach us and to lead us to faith in the Lord Jesus Christ, who is the fulfillment of the Law and the Prophets of the Old Testament.

> Do not think that I came to abolish the Law or the Prophets; I did not come to abolish but to fulfill. Matthew 5:17

Remember that the Word of the Lord stands forever (Isa. 40:7–8). Not one bit of it will ever pass away (Matt. 5:18–19, 24:35). Therefore, Jesus Christ, and His life within us, is the fulfillment of Old Testament Scripture.

With that in mind, let's look at some Old Testament passages that reveal the heart of God and His desire for us to be obedient. Mark your book if you need to because you will want to see what it is that God wants you to do and why. There is a reason for obedience, and our obedience to God will always lead to intimacy with Him. These verses are not the *letter* of the Law but the *heart* of the Law. See also if you can see where following God's Law leads to a saving faith in Jesus Christ.

> Oh that they had such a heart in them, that they would fear Me and *keep* all My commandments always, that it may be well with them and with their sons forever! Deuteronomy 5:29

> So you shall observe to *do* just as the LORD your God has commanded you; you shall not turn aside to the right or to the left. You shall *walk in all the way* which the LORD your God has commanded you, that you may live and that it may be well with you, and that you may prolong your days in the land which you shall possess. Deuteronomy 5:32–33

> Now this is the commandment, the statutes and the judgments which the LORD your God has commanded me to teach you, that you might *do* them in the land where you are going over to possess it, so that you and your son and your grandson might fear the LORD your God, to keep all His statutes and His commandments which I command you, all the days of your life, and that your days may be prolonged. O Israel, you should listen and be careful to do it, that it may be well with you and that you may multiply

greatly, just as the LORD, the God of your fathers, has promised you, in a land flowing with milk and honey. Deuteronomy 6:1–3

Here is the promise of a blessed life on earth when we trust His Word to obey it. The blessed life on earth comes with God's holy presence and intimacy with Him. Ultimately, those of us who trust and follow Christ will experience the epitome of intimacy, in His presence, for all eternity!

We have already discussed Joshua 1:8. This is my verse for intimacy with God. Just as a reminder, read it once again.

This book of the law shall not depart from your mouth, but you shall meditate on it day and night, so that you may be careful to do according to all that is written in it; for then you will make your way prosperous, and then you will have success. Joshua 1:8

When these things line up in my life, God graces me with His presence again and again in new and fresh ways. The key to intimacy with God is obedience.

NEW TESTAMENT

Now let's look at some New Testament Scriptures in the same way. I believe God's Word here is powerful and will speak to your heart without comments from me. The first verses are from the mouth of Jesus Christ Himself.

Not everyone who says to Me, 'Lord, Lord,' will enter the kingdom of heaven, but he who does the will of My Father who is in heaven. Matthew 7:21

Therefore everyone who hears these words of Mine and acts on them, may be compared to a wise man who built his house upon the rock. Matthew 7:24

[Teach] them to observe all that I commanded you; and lo, I am with you always, even to the end of the age. Matthew 28:20–21

But He said, "On the contrary, blessed are those who hear the word of God and observe it." Luke 11:28

If you know these things, you are blessed if you do them. John 13:17

Let me slip one more verse in before we move on.

Therefore, to one who knows the right thing to do and does not do it, to him it is sin. James 4:17

THE OBEDIENCE OF FAITH

There are many verses that could be shared on this subject, but I pray that these are enough to make your heart sensitive to obeying God.

In the Old Testament, obedience to God was crucial to the relationship. Man's obedience to God allowed him to maintain an intimate relationship with God. When the command of God was broken, the judgment of God came upon man, as we have seen in the story of King Saul. We see the impact of obedience very clearly in the relationship between God and Abraham. Genesis 22:18 says that because Abraham obeyed God, he would be blessed, and Abraham's blessing was that all the nations would be blessed through him: "In your seed all the nations of the earth shall be blessed, because you have obeyed My voice."

Through God's blessing on Abraham and through his lineage, our Savior, Jesus Christ, would come to earth. Eventually, the New Testament church would be born! Can you see now how significant Abraham's obedience was? Now look at the New Testament commentary on Genesis 22:18. "The Scripture, foreseeing that God would justify the Gentiles by faith, preached the gospel beforehand to Abraham, saying 'ALL THE NATIONS SHALL BE BLESSED IN YOU.' So then those who are of faith are blessed with Abraham, the believer'" (Gal. 3:8–9).

Abraham trusted God and placed His faith in God alone. His faith was not in Isaac or some future descendent. It was placed in God and His promises. Abraham's obedience is a blessing to us today. You go, Abraham! Hold nothing back! Again let me remind you, obedience to God through faith in God and His Word takes us to intimacy with God.

While Abraham is a wonderful example of faithful obedience in the Old Testament, the New Testament shows us our supreme example in Jesus Christ. Because of Christ's obedience to the Father, we can know the eternal source of salvation, which is a gift of God's grace to us. Christ held nothing back and was completely, sacrificially, perfectly obedient to the Father.

Obedience to Christ is our supreme act of faith. New Testament writers used phrases like "the obedience of faith" (Rom. 1:5) and "obedient children" (1 Peter 1:14). Author Walter G. Clippinger says it this way: "Thus it is seen that the test of fellowship with Yahweh in the Old Testament is obedience. The bond of union with Christ in the New Testament is obedience through faith, by which they become identified and the believer becomes a disciple."

LIVING OUT OUR FAITH

A friend of mine once said that if he could only live out the book of James, he would be right with God. And he was speaking the truth. The book of James gives us a full picture of what faith looks like. You see here the relationship between faith, or biblical belief, and obedience. Faith obeys the Word of God, and faith proves itself by works. It is our responsibility to apply the Word to our lives and let it have the transforming effect that it has the power to bring.

> But prove yourselves doers of the word, and not merely hearers who delude themselves. For if anyone is a hearer of the word and not a doer, he is like a man who looks at his natural face in a mirror; for once he has looked at himself and gone away, he has immediately forgotten what kind of person he was. But one who looks intently at the perfect law, the law of liberty, and abides by it, not having become a forgetful hearer but an effectual doer, this man will be blessed in what he does. James 1:22–25

Here we are challenged to prove ourselves to be doers of the Word and not merely hearers. The mere hearer deludes himself, says the Word of God. James tells us that looking into the Word of God and not allowing it to change us is like looking into a mirror, then walking away and not remembering what you looked like. That's not good! Think about it. A mirror will always bring about a change. If we are honest, and look long enough and deep enough, we will find that there is always something to add or subtract. If we walk away and forget to *respond* to what we have seen in the mirror, then we live with deception. (I am writing this at 6 AM. I have been to the mirror and I did not respond obediently to what it told me. Trust me, I am living with deception right now, but I will fix it when I am done with this chapter. Go on girl! Let the mirror speak!)

You know the story of Snow White. The wicked witch went to the mirror for the truth and the mirror told her the truth, but she didn't like what she heard. She tried to alter what she had heard, and her end was doom. The mirror does not lie. For now, consider the mirror as a symbol of the Word of God. It will always speak the truth and call for a change. The final result is based on our response.

The Word says that we are not to delude ourselves. The word *delude* means to mislead or deceive. I love that. Don't be misled or deceived in this discussion. Open your heart and let God's words speak truth to it.

Verse 25 tells us to look intently at the perfect law of liberty and abide by it. To *look intently* means to bend down low in order to take a close view, an intense survey, making no mistake about what you see. The word *perfect* means complete. God's law and His Word are complete. They are not going to change. They are forever settled.

Liberty does not mean our own will. True liberty is living as we should, not as we please. *As we should* means in obedience to God and His Word. *As we please* is anything less.

Abiding by the Word is simply allowing the Holy Scripture to be at home in our hearts. We are living by the Word that has taken permanent residence within us.

Living this way is living with the freedom that Christ brought to us through His cross, where He destroyed the power of sin and disobedience over our lives. We are no longer forgetful hearers, but effectual doers. Now, according to God's word, we are blessed in whatever we do, because we are doing the Word, which is the will of God.

God's blessing comes with His presence, and in His presence there is unprecedented intimacy. The whole purpose of this discussion and our living this way is that we might know the presence of God. You have seen it over and over again. His presence and His blessing come when we are faithfully obedient to *do* His word.

PERFECT FAITH

One final section from the book of James will lead us into the closing section of our discussion of obedience. Once again, the book of James gives us a very clear picture of genuine faith, and we have already seen that faith obeys the Word. If faith is the key to intimacy with God, then obedience is the power that turns the key, unlocking the way to intimacy with God.

In this final section, I want you to see that faith also proves itself by works. Our key witness is once again Abraham. I want you to see for yourself what the Scripture says about Abraham's sacrifice. I just know that these words from James 2:20–24 will lead us to a more genuine faith in the Lord Jesus Christ.

> But are you willing to recognize, you foolish fellow, that faith without works is useless? James 2:20

Ask yourself that question. Have you come to know that faith without works is useless? Do you say that you have faith, but there is no evidence in your life that faith exists? Verse 20 is very clear. Don't be foolish. Faith without works is foolish. Now watch what James says as he defends his point.

> Was not Abraham our father justified by works when he offered up Isaac his son on the altar? James 2:21

The implied answer to this question is "yes." The word *justified* means "declared righteous." Look at Abraham. He was justified when he offered up his son Isaac on the altar. His offering of Isaac was an expression of faith. True faith is made complete or full-grown when it is expressed in action.

I have studied three kinds of faith from the Bible. These New Testament definitions include *saving* faith, where at one moment in time one comes into a saving or salvation knowledge of God. There is also a *sanctifying* or sustaining faith, which comprehends the knowledge of God through identification with Jesus Christ, and one experiences God at work in his or her life. More simply stated, it is knowing God and appropriating His power in the experiences of our lives. Thirdly, there is *serving* or *obedient* faith, which acts upon the truths of God and His Son Jesus Christ as the Spirit of God enables and empowers through gifts of service. Faith is complete or perfected when we see this circle of faith in our day-to-day experience.

With that in mind, what we see is a *saving* faith in Genesis 15 made perfect through *serving* faith in Genesis 22 and James 2. That is exactly what James wrote in the following verse. I'll tell ya. Just keep reading and studying and allow the Scripture to reveal itself. You will find most of your answers in the Word. Between Genesis chapters 15 and 22, we will see Abraham's *sanctifying* faith. The following verses explain exactly what happened in Abraham's life.

> You see that faith was working with his works, and as a result of the works, faith was perfected; and the Scripture was fulfilled which says, "And Abraham believed God, and it was reckoned to him as righteousness," and he was called the friend of God. You see that a man is justified by works and not by faith alone. James 2:22–24

Genuine saving faith is always perfected by works. We are not justified, or declared righteous, just by saying that we belong to God. We are justified by our faith proving itself through works. We would do well to memorize these verses and ask God to help us live what we say we believe. Listen again to verse 24: "A man is justified by works, and not by faith alone."

We believe in Jesus Christ. We experience Him and serve Him. This is the complete picture of salvation. Stop at any point and you miss intimacy with God. We have to look at the whole counsel of God on any and every subject to get the full truth of what God is telling us. We cannot isolate our definitions and beliefs to one passage, not when God gives us more. I am not speaking at all of a salvation by works, but I am speaking about a salvation *that* works! Salvation comes from God's grace, accepted by a true faith. A true, authentic faith demonstrates itself by what it does.

The Friend of God

Did you see the phrase in verse 23, "and he [Abraham] was called the *friend of God*"? Abraham's obedience, the perfecting of his faith, gained him the title and the relationship, "friend of God." What kind of friendship was this? It was a covenant friendship! Abraham was identified with God and God distributed His life and His blessings upon Abraham, just as He had promised.

When Jesus called His disciples into covenant friendship, He called them to obedience. Jesus said, "You are My friends if you do what I command you" (John 15:14).

> No longer do I call you slaves, for the slave does not know what his master is doing; but I have called you friends, for all things that I have heard from My Father I have made known to you. You did not choose Me but I chose you, and appointed you that you would go and bear fruit, and

that your fruit would remain, so that whatever you ask of
the Father in My name He may give to you.
John 15:15–16

The relationship Jesus had with His disciples was intimate, deep, thorough, and personal. This is what we all
want with God. We want His presence. We want Him to
walk and talk with us. We want covenant friendship with
Him. And He wants the same. As we are obedient to Him,
we will experience this kind of intimacy with God.

I WILL LOVE YOU

Abraham became the friend of God. He enjoyed the presence of God, the blessing of God, and an intimate relationship with God. You and I can know and enjoy the
same relationship with a loving, promise-keeping God.
Look at what Jesus says in John 14:21:

He who has My commandments and keeps them is the
one who loves Me; and he who loves Me will be loved by
My Father, and I will love him and will disclose Myself to
him.

Jesus says our obedience to God's commands proves our
love for Him. He discloses three wonderful truths that
should be the desire of all of our hearts.

Jesus says when we prove our love for Him by keeping
His commands, we will be loved by the Father, Jesus Himself will love us, and He will disclose Himself to us. That is
the deepest intimacy we will ever know with God this side
of Heaven, and it is ours through simple obedience. Know
the Word, experience the Word, and keep the Word.

The real gem for me in this verse is the word *love*. The
Greek word used here is *agape*, which means to love deeply.

Our obedience will prove our deep love for God, and we can expect to receive in return God's deep love, revealed to us through His Son, our Beloved Savior, Jesus Christ. This is intimacy. This is true worship.

Chapter Four

Process of Sacrifice

I have some days when everything seems to be a major process. Nothing happens quickly, nothing has a bottom line, everything is a process. Just this morning I got up and was going to put on some very casual clothes so that I could go to the mall and do some major shopping. I wanted to be comfortable and not too fancy, so I thought, jeans and a sweatshirt, tennis shoes, and I am out the door. Because I was going to a nice mall, I did not want to wear a baseball cap. That would mean, according to the "mirror, mirror on the wall," completely doing my hair and face before going to the mall. With that, the process began. I was hoping to be ready in about thirty minutes, but once the process kicked in, it took me two hours! I cannot even tell you what distracted me, but when I was finally ready to go, two hours had passed, and the truth is, I was too tired to go to the mall. But I went anyway.

The process! I hate the process. It seems that every time I need a reimbursement check, I have to wait for weeks. I don't get it. Well, I know there is a process in place that must be carried out before a check can be cut. I understand that. I just don't like it.

Buying a car or a house is such a hassle because of the process. I must have signed 100 papers before the builder gave me the keys to our house at the closing. The process of closing took hours, and I hear that it could have been worse.

So just what is a process? Webster says that a process is the course of being done, the continuing development involving many changes. Yuk! Who has time in this day and age for the process? Come on, we live in a world of drive-thru windows and microwave ovens, electronic tickets and Internet shopping. Overnight it, will ya? Or better yet, put it on an airplane and get it here on the next flight. E-mail it to me or fax it to me, just don't make me wait. I don't have time for the process!

Well, this is the way about ninety percent of my day is spent. Hurry and wait. I seem to always be in a hurry, but I find myself always having to wait as well. The drive-thru line is so long that it has now turned into a process. Think about it: Order here. Pay here. Get your food here. Put your trash here. You know what? I'm outta here!

Now the microwave instructions are too detailed. Even the line for electronic tickets is long. (But that process really is one of the best and fastest.) The technology behind the Internet and e-mail and faxing is great, when it works. But when it is not working, it seems like my world comes to a screeching halt, or at best crawls along, and the process gets longer and longer.

I want everything now, yet my entire life has been characterized with having to go through the process, and then having to wait. I was thirty-four years old when I got married. I had my first baby at age thirty-seven and my second at thirty-nine. Now I'm forty!

Yet waiting has taught me the value of process. I am learning to appreciate the lessons I learn every step along the way. I have even come to enjoy the process because each lesson and victory along the way gives me strength and faith for the challenges yet to come. The process has become a trail of victory, and looking back gives me encouragement for today and all of my tomorrows.

Becoming a mother has taught me the greatest lesson on enjoying the process. Even though there are tough days during pregnancy, I am thankful for healthy pregnancies. I didn't want my babies to be born even one day before their little processes were complete inside of me. Now I didn't want them to be born early, but I most definitely did not want them to be born late. I had things to do! I have to go, go, go!

I have enjoyed the process of becoming one in heart with my husband. Of course, this will go on until one of us goes to be with the Lord, but our journey of falling in love day by day has been and still is a very sweet one. Overcoming the hurdles, which really are personality conflicts, has made the love more real and committed.

You should be there sometimes to watch this process. It is like North-and-South-and-never-the-twain-shall-meet. But we did meet, and we fell in love. Now this Southern girl and this Eastside Manhattan Yankee must work at becoming one in heart.

We do very well . . . until baseball season. Then Richard lets me choose where I want to watch the game, and he goes in the opposite direction. The rule is, when the game is over, the victor has to show love and kindness and sportsmanship to the one who has suffered the humiliation of defeat. Let me tell you, we are both terrible sports! The victor always rubs it in and does a silly little dance in the presence of the wounded. If the Yankees or Mets play another World Series, I may have to move to a hotel for a few days.

Nevertheless, somehow in the midst of Richard's victory dance, he manages to scoop me up and dance with me. I resist at first, but being close to him helps me overcome the disappointment of my team losing to his team, as long as I am winning with him. So I join him in the dance, and pretty soon we both forget all about the game. He forgets his victory and I forget my defeat. Now it's just the two of us—back in love and focused on each other.

Dying to myself and striving to bring Richard joy enables me to regard him as a cherished possession. I now describe that sweet man with just one word—mine! If you need more of a description I will use two words—all mine!

Yes, the process can be wearying, but when we let it do what it is intended to do, we end up with greater strength and assurance for the challenges that lie ahead. So let whatever process you are in take its course. You will end up with greater joy, strength, and peace.

PROCESS DELAYED

Now if you are like I am, already a little frustrated with the process, then you really are not going to like it when the process is delayed. The one delay that really tests my faith is an airport delay. I fly almost every week of the year, and a delay is the most dreaded part of my travels. But I have learned to be thankful for delays, as I remember that the airline is doing all they can to ensure my safety. Thank you! Yes, the process may experience a delay, but God is still sovereignly reigning during the delay.

I realized this while listening to a friend teach on the life of Abraham. I took the best notes I could, and after the meeting I ran for my Bible study help books. I found exactly what she found, of course. Once again I learned to appreciate the process, even if I am experiencing a temporary delay.

As you will know by now, Abraham is our star witness throughout this book. He was a great man of faith. But he did not start out that way. Abraham grew in his faith and obedience, just as you and I are growing. When he was called to make the sacrifice of Isaac, he drew strength from his journey. Abraham had been prepared through a life process.

It is very important for us to remember this because we are all in a process, and the process is for our safety; it is also for our good. Like father Abraham, we must allow ourselves to grow during the process and remember that God is in total control of it all.

If you have read only Genesis 12—where many consider the story of Abraham to begin—you may think that God spoke to Abraham and that he immediately and in full faith followed God in obedience. If you have read only Hebrews 11:8, you might think the same thing. However, as you look at all the related Scriptures and take a moment to examine it closely, you will find something else. Abraham was a teachable man, a man who grew in his faith and obedience. The process you see in his life will give you hope for your own journey.

I believe the delay in Abraham's obedience is recorded in Genesis 12:1: "Now the LORD had said unto Abram, Get thee out of thy country, and from thy kindred, and from thy father's house, unto a land that I will show thee" (KJV).

This verb tense, "had said," reveals to us that the Lord had spoken to Abram some time in the past. Look at the commentary from Acts, then we will move on. "And he said, 'Hear me, brethren and fathers! The God of glory appeared to our father Abraham when he was in Mesopotamia, before he lived in Haran'" (Acts 7:2). God had appeared to Abram before he lived in Haran. In Genesis 12:4, Abram leaves from Haran: "So Abram went forth as the LORD had spoken to him; and Lot went with him."

So why was Abraham delayed in obeying God and receiving the promises of God? Abraham's story actually begins in Genesis 11. Verse 31 tells us that before Abraham could leave Mesopotamia, where God had first spoken to him, Abraham was seized by his father and taken to Haran.

> Terah took Abram his son, and Lot the son of Haran, his grandson, and Sarai his daughter-in-law, his son Abram's wife; and they went out together from Ur of the Chaldeans in order to enter the land of Canaan; and they went as far as Haran, and settled there. Genesis 11:31

Note a few definitions and we will move on. The word *took* means to lay hold of, or to seize. Perhaps Abram's father took Abram by the arm and led him and the entire family toward Canaan, the place where God had told Abram to go, *without* his family.

Can we do a "what if"? What if Abram told his dad about the great promise of blessing that God had spoken to him, and Dad, who was an idolater (Josh. 24:2), decided that he wanted to get in on the act, add another "god" to his life, and head toward Canaan. Makes sense, but I will be careful to say that the Bible does not say why Terah headed toward Canaan.

Nevertheless, on their way to Canaan, under Terah's supervision, they stopped in Haran, a great city for business and trade in that day (not to be confused with Lot's father, who was named Haran). There they settled. The word *settled* means to dwell, to remain. If you are a Bible student you know that *to abide* means to be at home with. Terah made Haran home for his family.

I believe that Abram was delayed in Mesopotamia because he lacked encouragement from others to follow the Lord and because God's Word was not yet at home in Abram's heart. It is so very important that in our walk with the Lord, especially early on, we surround ourselves with godly people. They will help us and encourage us toward obedience and intimacy with God. Abraham had to grow in his relationship with God. Abraham had to learn through life's experiences, sovereignly orchestrated by God, that God will "operate when we co-operate." When God speaks, He really does expect us to trust what He says and obey fully and immediately.

Yet God understands better than we do that we are in a process that will continue until our mortality puts on immortality. Second Peter 3:18 says, "But grow in the grace and knowledge of our Lord and Savior Jesus Christ." *Knowledge* or *gnosis* is a learned knowledge. Intimacy is a process. We are to continue to grow in grace and in a learned knowledge of God through His holy Word applied in the everyday circumstances of our lives.

Second Peter 3:2 says, "that you should remember the words spoken beforehand by the holy prophets and the commandment of the Lord and Savior spoken by your apostles." *Old and New Testament.* We are to let all of the Word of God dwell richly within us, then we will have good success.

There was an old preacher in my dad's church who would always say, "It takes time to be holy." He was right. The process of salvation is a lifelong one. Like you and me, Abraham would have to grow in grace and in the knowledge of His God. Abraham was delayed in receiving the promises of God because as the patriarch of the family, Abraham's dad still had a prominent place in Abraham's heart.

Most people have trouble letting go of some things, and I would think that family would be the hardest. But look at what Jesus says to those of us who would follow Him and know Him intimately. "If anyone comes to Me, and does not hate his own father and mother and wife and children and brothers and sisters, yes, and even his own life, he cannot be My disciple" (Luke 14:26).

Man! I mean Girl! . . . Or whoever is reading this! Those are very strong words. What is the message in Jesus' statement? *Hate* here means to love to a lesser degree. Jesus, who is God, says that we are to love God first, more, and best of all. If we do not, He says we cannot be His disciples.

Those are strong words but powerful and sweet, because Jesus is God, and nothing and no one in our lives could even begin to compare with all He is.

Are you delayed in receiving God's promises in your life? Are you "slipping and sliding in the same old mud, never seeming to advance"? If you are, then go before the Lord and be very honest with Him. Ask God to show you why there is a delay. Ask Him to show you what it is in your life that keeps you away from what He has for you. Ask Him to show you how to advance and know intimacy with Him.

We know that God is sovereign and works in His own time to fulfill His purposes in each of us (Ecc. 3:11). Yet He could be waiting for us to obey what He has last spoken to us, so that He can get us on over into the land of promise.

So hold nothing back. Hold nothing so close to your heart or in your hands that it keeps you away from the *promises* you have in Christ Jesus. "For as many as are the *promises* of God, in Him *they* are yes; therefore also through Him is our Amen to the glory of God through us" (2 Cor. 1:20).

Don't be delayed. Make the necessary sacrifices, and let sacrificial obedience lead you into the blessings of God, and intimacy with Him.

HELD UP IN HARAN

Abraham got delayed. We don't know how long, but at the end of verse 31 of Genesis 11, we find Abraham *held up in Haran!* We know that they were headed for Caanan, but I guess they got side tracked by the hustle and bustle of Haran.

Haran was a metropolitan city in the day of Abraham. Lots of business and trade were there. We do not know the details of the "Abrams" while they lived there, but I can imagine that city life was probably good to them.

One of my dreams is to live on 5th Avenue in New York City. I want to live in a high rise condo over-looking Central Park. Now for me, that would be the life. I would busy my days with all the "good" stuff that New York has to offer.

My husband is from New York City, lower Eastside Manhattan, and he says it would take a major clear word from God for him to move back. I guess he knows the good, the bad, and the ugly of it all. All I know is that I understand Eva Gabor's part in the "Green Acres" song: "Darling I love you, but give me Park Avenue."

I guess I just have to thank God for a husband who is willing to obey God and follow His command. Alabama has been good to us! Roger Breland (an Alabamian), founder of TRUTH and like a dad to me, would always say, "If the devil can't make you bad, he will make you busy."

I can easily imagine why Abram's family settled in Haran. Haran had everything that they thought they wanted and needed, so they settled there until Terah, Abram's father, died.

Stop and think for a moment how easy it is to get off the path of obedience. How easy is it to get distracted by the good things that the world has to offer? Every time I go to New York, I want to put a stake in the ground.

If we get to a place that has "all we ever wanted," we could easily think that "this is where God wants me to be." It is easy to settle there and make that place our home.

How many have gotten to Haran, near the kingdom of God, but failed to get to Caanan, the land of promise?

Check this out. Esther was offered half the kingdom (Esther 5:6). God has promised to give us the *kingdom*. "Do not be afraid, little flock, for your Father has chosen gladly to give you the kingdom" (Luke 12:32). Which would you rather have? What is the prerequisite for gaining the kingdom? "But seek first His kingdom and His righteousness, and all these things will be added to you" (Matt. 6:33).

Far too many times I have settled for good and not for God. I too have been held up in Haran! I really have determined that I do not want to live like this any more. I no longer want only *good* things, I want *God* things. I don't want to settle in Haran; I want the blessings of Caanan.

Let me get personal for a minute. Too many of you are settling because "your biological clock is ticking!" Don't fall for a lie. Time is your friend. I should know. I did not get married until I was 34. Our first son was born when I was 37. I thank God that our second son was born a month before I turned 40!

I have a dear friend who was married for the first time at 57! Her man was, I think, 59! They both looked like they were about 25 when they got married. I kid you not. Neither had children, and neither had been married before. I know that the older you get, the harder it seems to find Mr. Right, but God has a plan. The issue is good vs. God. Don't settle until you get to the "God" thing in your life. The greatest enemy to that which is *best* for you is often something that is *good*.

Abram was held up in Haran! He was distracted by the good, which, for the moment, kept him from God's best.

Sidebar! Have you ever heard the phrase *God's Word is settled*? That means it is finished. It is *not going to change*.

His Word, which is His will for you, is not going to change. His desire for you is for good and not for calamity. "'For I know the plans that I have for you,' declares the LORD, 'plans for welfare and not for calamity to give you a future and a hope'" (Jer. 29:11).

For me, it is exciting . . . no . . . it is elation to discover God's will for me in any given situation. To discover His will is to know intimacy with Him. Nothing, absolutely nothing, compares with that.

You may say, "Alicia, I'm just not there. I don't get the God thing like you do." Then know that I am praying for you, because I know that when you "get it," you will never want to let it go!

My heart is always troubled when someone shares with me what he or she believes God's will is in any given circumstance. As I listen, I am listening for the Word of God in that person's life, and most times that person has been everywhere except to God's holy Word. Let me remind you that when you open your Bible, God opens His mouth. Start there. He has promised to instruct us and teach us in the way we should go. He has promised to guide us with His eyes upon us (Psalm 32:8). Also remember Joshua 1:8.

We have hope in Christ that enables us to decide today to live differently. God has already given us everything we need for life and godliness through a deep, relational knowledge of the Lord Jesus Christ (2 Peter 1:3). Life is in the Word, and we would do amazingly well to embrace the Word and allow it to guide us through the process of life.

Don't get held up with the good and miss God. It is time to obey the Word of the Lord and get on over into Canaan.

Here is a statement from Eleanor Roosevelt that will really help put all this into perspective. Ms. Eleanor said, "One's philosophy is not best expressed in words. It is expressed in the choices one makes. In the long run, we shape our lives and we shape ourselves. The process never ends until we die. And the choices we make are ultimately our responsibility."

Sacrificial obedience will lead to intimacy with God, and right now, in Abram's life, though it was early in his walk with the Lord, he was likely missing that intimacy. Not to worry, Abram, you will have a hundred more years to get it right (Gen. 25:7).

ON THE ROAD AGAIN

Eventually, Abram headed out of Haran and into the land of promise. He was still not sure where he was going, but he had grown in his faith. He headed out of his own country and left most of his family.

Let's review what God said to Abram while he and his family were in Ur:

> Now the LORD said to Abram, "Go forth from your country, and from your relatives and from your father's house, to the land which I will show you; and I will make you a great nation, and I will bless you, and make your name great; and so you shall be a blessing; And I will bless those who bless you, and the one who curses you I will curse. And in you all the families of the earth will be blessed." Genesis 12:1–3

What a great Word from God! Seven promises came out of one intimate moment with God:
1. "I will make you a great nation."
2. "I will bless you."
3. "I will make your name great."
4. "You will be a blessing."
5. "I will bless those who bless you."

6. "Whoever curses you I will curse."
7. "All people on earth will be blessed through you."

All Abram had to do was faithfully obey God, and he would be the most blessed man on the face of the earth. Wouldn't you love it if God spoke that to you? Nevertheless, Abram's obedience required a great sacrifice on his part. He had to leave his country, but more importantly, he had to leave his family.

God had chosen Abram and Sarai to be the beginning of a holy nation, set apart, which God would raise up for Himself. They were the beginning of God's plan for the redemption of all mankind. So at the age of seventy-five, Abram left Haran and headed for the land of Canaan.

Let me stop here and encourage you to read this wonderful passage of Scripture. Please read Genesis 12 and 13 and allow God to show you His truth.

Abram was headed in the right direction. He traveled on until he reached Shechem, and there the Lord told Abram, "To your offspring I will give this land." So Abram built an altar there to the Lord. Abram moved on to Bethel, and there he built another altar and called on the name of the Lord. He grew in his relationship with God.

But there was a famine in Bethel, which means "house of God." There was no bread in the house of God. I'm sure he must have thought, "Nope! This does not look like a blessing to me. I'm outta here." So Abram journeyed on.

Have you ever gotten to a place where God had told you to go, and found that there was a famine? Did you look up and say "Huh-uh, this ain't the right place, God. I do not see any blessing in this. I must have missed what You said. I guess I'll keep going until I get to something that makes a little more sense to me."

Abram went as far south as Egypt. Abram, Sarai, Lot, and the whole bunch were moving south. Abram was not about to settle his family in a land of famine, so he moved on to Egypt, where he then lied about his relation to Sarai. He lied in order to save his own life because his princess-wife Sarai was so beautiful. He was afraid the Egyptians would kill him and take her. He told them that she was his sister. And she was, in fact, his half-sister. But the lady was also his wife. That would have meant more to the Pharaoh than knowing that Sarai was Abram's sister!

The Egyptian servants believed him and took Sarai to Pharaoh. And Abram got what he wanted: food. He also got sheep and cattle, male and female donkeys, menservants and maidservants, and camels.

Meanwhile, he did not know what was happening to Sarai. If I were in Sarai's position, I would have been thinking of ways to get back at him. Perhaps she was!

But God inflicted serious diseases on Pharaoh and his household because Sarai was Abram's wife. They discovered this and let her go back to Abram. They also let Abram keep all that they had given him.

So you see, father Abraham had a rough start to his journey. He got some things very right and some things very wrong.

Perhaps you have lost your way or are held up by some delay. Are you in the land of promise with nowhere to settle, so you just journey on? This is how I feel a lot of the time. Many times I feel like I am in the right place, but I am circling, looking for the perfect place to land. This just makes a long trip even longer.

Let me encourage you to remember the last thing that God spoke to you. Do that and God will speak to you again. You will make mistakes. God will not wipe you out for making a mistake. He knows you better than you know yourself, and He still has a wonderful plan for your life.

BUILDING ALTARS

One of the right things that Abram did during his process—something important that you and I must do—is to build altars. What I mean is marking important moments and experiences with God so we never forget them. These altars or markers are between God and us, yet sometimes they are visible for others to see, so that they take notice of who God is and what He does in a life obedient to Him. Once he entered the land of Canaan, Abram built altars in places where he had memorable spiritual experiences. By building altars, Abram acknowledged that the land of Canaan belonged to the Lord.

The Old Testament word for *altar* means a place of slaughter or sacrifice. However, Old Testament altars were not restricted to animal sacrifices but were used for other purposes as well. Joshua 22:26–27 shows us that altars were sometimes used as memorials of the Israelite heritage or to bring into remembrance a particular major event:

> Therefore we said, "Let us build an altar, not for burnt offering or for sacrifice; rather it shall be a witness between us and you and between our generations after us, that we are to perform the service of the LORD before Him with our burnt offerings, and with our sacrifices and with our peace offerings, so that your sons will not say to our sons in time to come, 'You have no portion in the LORD.'"

I am writing this book just a few months after the terrorist attacks on the World Trade Center in New York City. The question now is, "What do we build next?" Some would like to see the buildings rebuilt so that terrorists see our resilience and lack of fear. Others would like to see a memorial put there as a reminder of the event so that we are never caught off guard again.

Just recently I visited the memorial in Oklahoma City, where the Alfred P. Murrah Federal Building once stood.

It is now a place of remembrance of those who lost their lives there and of the sorrow felt by the families who lost loved ones. There is an incredible statue of a weeping Lord Jesus over the tragedy that took place there. The memorial is beautiful, and I believe it captures the emotion of what happened that day and the deep sorrow that still lingers.

When I went to Israel and saw the memorials to the Jewish people who had lost their lives in the Holocaust, I wanted to fall on my knees and ask God why. My heart broke for them and for others who have suffered so terribly. Memorials such as these cause us to remember certain events and help us live stronger and more guarded lives in the future.

In the Atlanta airport is a memorial to Dr. Martin Luther King, Jr. and his work for civil rights here in America. He was much more than just a man with a mission. He was a man called, stirred, and empowered by the all-powerful God, Jehovah.

Old Testament altars were also built as reminders of the Israelite heritage. This is what Abram built as he entered the land of Canaan.

> The LORD appeared to Abram and said, "To your descendants I will give this land." So he built an altar there to the LORD who had appeared to him. Genesis 12:7

This is significant because we see that rather early in Abram's walk with the Lord, he was developing as a true worshiper. He would need good altar-building skills later in his life. God was sovereignly teaching him the importance of worship.

This is important also because worship is a response to truth. Now you see Abram responding more immediately to the word of the Lord. He was in a process and he was growing.

In response to God's promise, "To your descendants I will give this land," Abram built an altar at Shechem, aligning himself with the will of God. He declared that the land did indeed belong to the Lord and that the Lord was giving it to Abram and his descendents as an everlasting inheritance.

Abram journeyed on through the land, and built an altar at Bethel and Ai (Gen. 12:8) and one at Hebron (Gen. 13:18), calling on the name of the Lord. The last altar that we see Abram building is on top of Mount Moriah; we will talk about that altar when we get there.

It was also important for Abram to build these altars because of what we see in Genesis 12:6: "Abram passed through the land as far as the site of Shechem, to the oak of Moreh. Now the Canaanite was then in the land."

The Canaanites were big-time idolaters and had built altars to idols all over the land. So when Abram got there and God told him that He was giving the land to him, his only response was to build an altar, serving the Canaanites notice that God was in the house.

So here was Abraham, in the beginning stages of his journey, or process, learning to set up mile markers, or landmarks, or altars; learning to respond immediately to the Word of the Lord so that he would remember and live by all that God had spoken.

This is a great way to recall a journey or process with the Lord. It is also a great way to live. We all need to set up reminders of God's Word all around us. We need to build altars that remind us of our own spiritual encounters with the Lord and of major events where He has shown Himself mighty to us.

Altars will strengthen us in the process. Even if there is a delay or famine or if there are enemies all around, when we go back to our altar and remember the promise of God, we will receive power and faith to continue the journey that God has carved out for us.

ALTARS TODAY

As I write this, I cannot help but think about the altars or markers that I have built along my own journey. I did not realize what I was doing at the time, but God has since shown me that my responses have been acts of worship. I have responded to the truth He has spoken to my heart, and have set up memorials, or landmarks, that remind me of those spiritual moments with the Lord.

I cannot begin to tell you all of them, but perhaps some of these will cause you to be reminded of spiritual moments you have had with the Lord.

I have a little diamond cross necklace that I have worn for the past ten years. It's a memorial. It is an altar. After being in the musical group TRUTH for six years, Mr. Breland, the director of the group, gave it to me as he gave his blessing on my new ministry. He said, "Here are six diamonds, for six years of TRUTH. Diamonds because you are no longer in the rough, and a cross because of your love for Christ." This is how he helped launch me into full-time Christian ministry.

That little cross is a reminder of more things than I can write in this book. It keeps me focused on who I am and what my purpose in life really is.

Richard and I have a statue of Moses holding up Holy Scripture. I have placed it over a picture of us. It looks great on our mantle, but its real purpose is for more than beauty. It reminds me daily that the final authority in our lives and in our marriage is the Word of God. God is the sovereign administrator of our covenant marriage. May the Lord watch between us. I will teach this to my children.

We also have a beautiful plaque of the Ten Commandments. We have Scripture beautifully framed in every room of our house. We have altars all around to remind us of the faithfulness of God and to strengthen us during our process.

Jeremiah 29:11 has been one of my favorite verses for years. I see it all over my house. It seems like just when I need it most, that verse stares at me and I am again helped in the process. God has a plan for me, and that plan is for my good.

Another great altar is our wedding video. We watch it every anniversary and are reminded of our commitment to each other. God spoke very powerfully at our wedding, and once a year we visit that altar and are reminded of what God said. Sobering!

It is also exciting and humbling to see the ways in which God has kept His promises to us. All the more should we keep our promises to Him and to each other. Perhaps we should watch that wedding video after we've watched a ball game!

I remember a time of prayer when God told me that my husband was a gift. My first silly thought was, "If it doesn't fit, can I exchange it?" Immediately God interrupted my thought with His powerful Word. He was not joking! He reminded me that He is the giver of good and perfect gifts, and He assured me that there would be no need for exchange! Recognize that God's gift of a spouse is something to continually give thanks to God for. Express your thanks to God and to your spouse for how God uses that person to make your life more complete.

I try to capture on film "God moments" and put them in an album so that when we tell the story of our family it becomes a God story. God did this and God did that. I have shared some of these stories with my friends, and I find that they are left dumbfounded by them. Well, these stories are all true. There is a God story in almost every-thing around us. I love to tell these God stories.

You may know the story of how God healed me of cer-vical cancer. My altar is the song "Healing." I sing this song and share that story as often as I can. Yes, I lost three friends to cancer while I was sick, but God wrote a differ-ent story in my book. He chose to heal me and charged me to tell others that He is still *Jehovah Rapha*, the God who heals! I thought I would never have children, and now I have two beautiful sons! These are the real "altar" boys!

I believe your Bible is an altar and you are the sacrifice. In the Word is where we die to self that we might live for God. Joshua 1:8 is an altar in my life. I have already told you that story. Genesis 17:1 is the altar I have built for this year. Thank you, God, for Your true, unfailing Word.

Will you build an altar daily and present yourself to God as a living sacrifice? If you will, He will in turn con-sume your life with the fire of His presence. You will know His ways, and His presence will go with you (Ex. 33:14). You will find deep intimacy with God.

Pain in the Process

I can remember a desperate time in my life when I wanted to kill myself. When I decided how I would do it, the sweet presence of Jesus came and said, "That will hurt." I laughed and laughed and laughed. He knows exactly what to say to me. He knows that I cannot stand pain. I just needed to be reminded of the pain. The way He dealt with me made me laugh at myself. What a wonderful Lord.

When I delivered my babies, I told the nurse to write "epidural" on every page of my chart. I threatened to order T-shirts and hats, streamers and balloons that all read "epidural!"

Yet I know that pain is a part of the process. Let's not do a whole chapter on the pain of sacrifice. I hate it too much. Pain is undoubtedly part of true sacrifice. You will see that throughout this book.

The giving of life is painful, but it brings forth new life. I can endure the pain of childbirth because I know what is on the other side of that pain. The painful sacrifice in my body has brought forth precious new life into the world. Praise the Lord.

Jesus Christ gave His life on the cross to bring forth new spiritual life in all of us. His cross was painful. Yet the reward is greater than the sacrifice. He would rather die than live without us. Oh, what love! What joyful pain of sacrifice!

I can handle discipline, the trial of my faith, because the trying of my faith develops patience and perseverance (James 1:2–4). Perseverance must finish its work so that I may be mature and complete, not lacking anything. Pain is a part of the process; it has a purpose, and that purpose is to make me complete in my faith.

Pain caused by a lack of faith or disobedience, I know, can be avoided. God's plan for me is not to go through that kind of pain. His plan is for good and not for evil (Jer. 29:11).

I Got Picked

One more story! I get a kick out of this one. I was reading my daily Bible portion and was finishing the story of Esther. Well, I do not know what came over me, but I saw the story of Esther from a perspective I never had before.

When I got to the end of the story of Esther, let's just say that I was *sick of Esther*! She had gotten everything! I felt like I was getting nothing! She was very content with

her life as an orphan with Mordecai. She was not out trying to serve God. She had not left her family and was not
stuck in Travelers Rest, South Carolina, for a week, with
no Starbucks, like I was! She had not left her husband and
son at home for the fiftieth time that year. She didn't have
any passion in her soul to do *great things for God!* She was
not making any sacrifices and she was not interested at all
in God's plan for her life. She was a good Jewish girl, and
that was enough for her.

I began talking to God and it went something like this:

"*Look at me, God!* I am out here working my fingers to
the bones, *for You*, and I get nothing. *Nothing!* I can't even
get a good Christian television station to help me while I
am away from home.

"What's up with Esther, anyway? How come You
picked her for beauty lessons for a year and marriage to the
king, who was willing to give her *half the kingdom?* She had
great clothes, a great house, servants—anything a girl
would dream of—and she didn't even ask for it.

"What good is it, God, for me to live for You and work
for You and make the sacrifices that I do if You are never
going to pick *me*? How can I sing the song 'We Win' when
I feel like such a loser?

"I believe I can see Your plan and purpose in my life. I
know what Your Word says, but why don't I see this stuff
happening in my life? And God, why is it so hard for those
I have asked to help me to catch a vision for this ministry?
They don't even seem to want to. Why is that, God? I
want my life to count for You. You say that I am to fulfill
my ministry. That is all I want to do. I don't mind the sacrifices. I can believe that I have been brought into the
kingdom for such a time as this, but I just don't see it right
now. If getting from one point to the next is this difficult,
maybe You are not in it. Maybe You are not helping me at

all. I'll quit right now if You want me to. I will pack my bags and go home if You are not going to help me. It's really and truly too hard right now. I have no more fight, no more strength, no more to give. If You are not going to help me, then I quit. This is just too hard. Your favor seems to always fall on someone else. I never get picked. I just get picked on."

About then I felt the sweet gracious presence of Jesus come to me. His presence this time was very much like it was when I finally got to a place in my heart where I could pray about my cancer. The difference, this time, is that He did not say a word.

Nevertheless, I knew that His presence was enough. At that moment my heart started to break. I was thrilled with just the nearness of God. I really did not need anything more. I realized vividly that I am a blessed lady, and that many women would love to change places with me.

I could not tell God that I was sorry for feeling the way I did, because my feelings were very real. I did tell Him, though, that if He never picked me, as long as I could sense His presence in what I was doing, I would keep going as long as He wanted me to. I thanked Him for the grace of His presence and went on with my day.

Well, that very day I was chosen to sing at a luncheon for the elderly. It was great. After lunch I went back to my hotel room and started back to work. I decided to return some phone calls. I called a gentleman in Houston, Texas, who said to me, "Alicia, we were considering who should lead worship at our International Conference in Hong Kong, and as we were considering several people, your name rose to the top of the list."

I got picked! I got picked! I thought. I told him I would need to pray about this. I held the phone away from my ear for about two seconds and then said, "Yes!" He gave me the details and I was filled with excitement.

Moments later I returned another call. My friend said, "Alicia, we were considering who should host our new television show, and out of several people your name rose to the top of the list."

This is the truth. They both said the exact same thing. This all happened within a thirty-minute time period.

Once again I said I would have to pray about this. I held the phone away again for about two seconds and then answered with a hearty "Yes!" He gave me the details, as much as he knew at that point. We will start production of the television show just as I finish this book.

When that conversation was over, I jumped up and down on both beds and screamed, "I got picked! I got picked!"

I called my cousin, Aleatha, who lives in Long Island, New York. She and a group of people up there are my prayer partners. They had been praying with me for months about our ministry's relationship with the TV station. We were not asking for a show, just for a good relationship so that I could make occasional appearances.

When I told her about the phone call, she screamed and said, "Hold on! I'm driving on the Long Island Expressway, and I gotta pull over and shout!"

She did.

We all need a cousin or friend like Aleatha.

I jumped and screamed and laughed and cried and jumped and screamed and laughed and cried.

That morning I was spiritually exhausted. I could not get to the next place in my process. So I took the wood off of my back and the fire out of my soul. I built an altar and placed myself on it. Jesus came and consumed me with the fire of His presence and reminded me that "Alicia Renée Williamson Garcia has been brought into the kingdom for such a time as this."

The name *Alicia* means "truthful." *Renée* means "born again." *Garcia* means "spear strong."

It is my delight and my will to serve the great I Am because of the great heritage I have in His Son.

What about You? Are you living for the King of Kings, called to a deeper place of worship, yet you find yourself held up in Haran? Are you inundated with enemies, yet are you building altars to serve them notice that you are God's possession and that your heritage is with Him?

Then press on, my friend. Take the wood off of your back and the fire from your soul. Build an altar and place yourself on it. Wait for God to come and consume your heart with the gracious fire of His presence. It is all a part of the process. You will find joy unspeakable, filled with glory. You will realize that you have been "picked," and that you are indeed chosen for such a time as this. You'll have to pull over and shout! You will jump and laugh and cry and jump and laugh and cry. Jump! Laugh! Cry!

> "For the vision is yet for the appointed time; it hastens toward the goal and it will not fail. Though it tarries, wait for it; for it will certainly come, it will not delay."
> Habakkuk 2:3

Chapter Five

Progress of Sacrifice

*D*o you remember progress reports? School report cards were stressful enough, but progress reports were even worse! They were like the steam before the boil, the wind before the storm. I hated them.

My mother, a public school teacher, would get my progress reports before the school day was out many times. Sometimes I would not get them at all. My teachers would give them to her so she was ready for me before I had a chance to pray. I did not even get the grace of prayer time on the bus after school. Trust me! I would have prayed on those days, for sure!

When I saw her she would look at me with those "Mother" eyes and ask, "Why did you get a B in math and a C in science?" At least I was smart enough not to be a wise gal with her. I would always take the "have mercy on me" route.

"I don't know, Mom. I tried really hard and did my best." Then I would blink hard and slow. My chin would drop and I would wear a really sad face.

It took my mom about two seconds to see beyond this charade, and she would always say, "Well, we (I never knew who "we" was) will just have to try a little harder, won't we!" She would never tell me that my best was not good enough, but the strong implication was that I should do better next time!

"Yes, Ma'am."

Now Dad was just the opposite. He thought a B in math and a C in science were pretty good for his little evangelist, Alicia. I could miss the number of divisions slightly and that would be acceptable. Science didn't matter because I would be serving the God of miracles, and you can't explain that stuff scientifically anyway! With Dad, I was doing great (smirk)!

My grades really were fine all through school. I graduated with honors from college, thank You, Lord! Nevertheless I always dreaded progress reports. I am just thankful that they always showed a little progress and hardly any regression. I excelled in some things, and others came a little slower. That was fine, too, because in the end, when it really mattered, I seemed to always make the grade!

Why is it that many of the things in life that we dread seem to be the most helpful to us? I don't know, and I don't think I really want to know. But again, just as every process has a place and a purpose, so does progress.

Progress is measured when there is a little pop-quiz along the journey. The quiz will show where you are in the process, where you excel and where you need to grow. It is for your good, and there is no getting around it.

We just walked with Abram through the early stages of his life and found that his growth was a process. Just like all of us, Abram did well in some areas and not so well in others. Nevertheless, we saw that he was very teachable and that he progressed through the process of faith development.

We won't examine his whole life (I know you're glad), but let's at least look at some of the key areas of his progress. Remember that Abraham is the father of the faith for those who believe in the Lord Jesus Christ, but his faith was developed over the course of his life.

One of my favorite verses about Abraham says that when he was called to sacrifice Isaac, he "reckoned" that God was able to raise the dead. That's big. That is really big because he had never seen or known God to do that before. He had seen God do extraordinary things, and he knew a lot about God's nature. So when God told him to sacrifice Isaac, he put precept upon precept and believed that God would raise up Isaac. This was a test to show Abraham's progress, and he got an A. He chose the right answer and—better than that—his faith was perfected by his works and he became the friend of God (James 2:23).

Isn't that what we want—friendship with God? We want faith that is perfected through the tests of life and a relationship with the Most High God, where He calls us His covenant friends. We don't have to dread a pop quiz or progress report. They are there to show us where we are in our love for and faith in God. God already knows where we are. He wants us to know, too, so that we will be encouraged to grow.

Fear not. If you are not making the grade in a particular area now, God will be merciful and will help you do better next time.

RIGHT CHOICES

I have to believe that Abram knew that God would help him in his faith, because even though he was missing the mark in his early walk with the Lord, he continued to grow and trust God for greater faith. Leaving his country was hard, but after a delay, he did just that. Leaving his family was even harder, but after awhile he was able to do that also. With every victory, Abram found more of the nearness of God and one victory always led to another.

One major victory that helped Abram begin to progress rapidly was finally separating from his nephew, Lot. I am sure that Lot was like a son to Abram because Haran, Lot's father and Abram's brother, had died when the family was still in Ur of the Chaldeans. Once they came to Canaan, their caravan was too large and the land would not sustain all of them in one place. The herdsmen began to argue over water and vegetation for the animals, and this displeased Abram greatly. So Abram lovingly asked Lot to separate from him. He even gave Lot the choice of where he wanted to live. Abram would simply go the other way.

Lot chose for himself the well-watered valley of the Jordan, and by the sovereign hand of God, Abram received the land of Canaan (Gen. 13:10–12). Now, for the first time since entering the land God showed him, we see that Abram finally settled in the land.

Abram obeyed God, and God spoke to him again (Gen. 13:14–18). Obedience brings intimacy.

No doubt Abram loved Lot and there probably was no natural reason for them to separate. But the land was not to be inherited by Lot. God was giving it to Abram and his descendents. God was beginning to separate for Himself a holy people.

Lot had to go. And when he did go, God spoke again to Abram, and Abram built an altar.

PROMOTION COMES FROM GOD

One other right choice that Abram made was the choice to allow his promotion to come from God and not from men. After Lot separated from Abram, there was a war. Lot was captured along with the entire city of Sodom. A servant escaped to tell Abram, the Hebrew, and Abram rallied his camp to rescue Lot from captivity (Gen. 14:11–14).

This is the first time Abram is called a "Hebrew" in the Word of God (vs. 13). So we now see that God is recognizing him and his camp as a separate people, a people called and set apart by God for divine purposes. At the end of the war, Abram was greeted by Melchizedek. Melchizedek was the king of Salem and a priest of the Most High God. The name Melchizedek means "king of righteousness."

Salem is probably a shorter form of the word "Jerusalem," and is related to the Hebrew word for peace. Melchizedek greeted Abram with bread and wine. The bread and wine constituted an ordinary meal, signifying graciousness and friendship. Melchizedek blessed Abram, saying, "Blessed be Abram of God Most High, possessor of heaven and earth; and blessed be God Most High, who has delivered your enemies into your hand" (Gen. 14:19–20).

El Elyon, or "God Most High," is another name for God. This Hebrew word means "sovereign." Melchizedek revealed to Abram more about the God that they both served. Abram now had a name for God: "Most High God." He also knew that this sovereign God was the One who had delivered his enemies into his hand. Recognizing that Melchizedek was the priest of the Most High God, Abram gave him an offering of one tenth of all that he had (Gen. 14:20).

The blessing and favor of God was the reason for Abram's success over his enemies, and he realized this now more than ever. Abram's faith in God was reflected in his response to the king of Sodom, who came to greet him after the war.

The king of Sodom proposed that Abram build an alliance with him by giving the people of Sodom back to him, and he offered for Abram to keep all of the goods.

Abram's response is priceless! He acted on what he had just learned about the God that he served. This was the response of a man who was growing in his faith and obedience. This was the response of an obedient worshiper of God.

Abram said to the king of Sodom, "I have sworn to the Lord God Most High, possessor of heaven and earth, that

I will not take a thread or a sandal thong or anything that is yours, for fear you would say, 'I have made Abram rich.' I will take nothing except what the young men have eaten, and the share of the men who went with me, Aner, Eshcol, and Mamre; let them take their share." Genesis 14:22–24

Abram recognized God as the sovereign ruler of his life, El Elyon, the creator and Lord of heaven of earth, Elohim. Because God is all of this, He does not need man's possessions and blessings. All Abram was and had came from the God he served.

Abram recognized rather early in his journey that promotion comes from God. Psalm 75:6–7 (KJV) says, "For promotion cometh neither from the east, nor from the west, nor from the south. But God is the judge: he putteth down one, and setteth up another."

If promotion is not from the east, nor the west, nor the south, then it must come from the north. North is where the throne of God is, and promotion comes from Him (Psalm 48:2).

Abram knew this and lived in response to this. Another right choice, Abram. A+! We will see the beautiful covenant blessing that followed this act of obedience.

My friends, there is a simple but great lesson here. It is what I call the "because God said so" answer. Abram had grown in his relationship with God and had just been blessed in the presence of the priest Melchizedek. His strength was in the Lord and his response to the king of Sodom was in response to his God—not to what an earthly king could give him.

Abram recognized that God had a sovereign purpose and plan for his life and that God would accomplish this plan in His own time and in His own way. He had learned through the process of growing that the world could offer him nothing that would cause him to grow in God or gain the promises of God. Growth and progress in the Lord come through faith in God alone.

And don't forget that faith without works is dead. Abraham was exercising the faith that he received from the words of Melchizedek. This is no case for poverty. God can and does use others to bless us so that we can build His kingdom. However, Abram recognized in this instance that he was to turn his attention to what the Most High God was giving him and not to what the earthly king had to offer. You and I must also live responding to "thus saith the Lord" so that we too will know when to say "yes" or "no" to the gifts that come from humankind. We must fill our lives with "God things" and not just "good things."

Abram chose the blessing of God—graciousness and friendship with God. He chose intimacy with God over material possessions. He had learned from the past and was living more wisely in the present. God would bless him greatly in the future for this act of obedience.

Do you have an offer before you because someone else can capitalize on a success that God has brought into your life? Be careful! Seek the Lord. Make sure that the offer is from the hand of God and not from one who is seeking personal profit from your gain. Don't sell out. Be sold-out to intimacy with God and His sovereign purpose and plan for your life. Now, on to the next event.

RECKONED AS RIGHTEOUS

After Abram gave an offering to Melchizedek and was challenged by the offer from the king of Sodom, an intimate moment with God followed. God came to Abram and spoke the secret, intimate things of the Lord, saying, "Do not fear, Abram, I am a shield to you; your reward shall be very great" (Gen. 15:1).

The war was over and God told Abram not to be afraid. God would continue to protect him, and—by the way—God did not forget His promise: Abram's reward was great.

Beginning in chapter 15, we see Abram going to another level in the Lord. His prayers were getting stronger and bolder. He knew more about God and he had faith to ask questions. It takes faith to ask God questions. But be warned! Before you ask, make sure you prepare your heart for His answers. He speaks in truth and His Word stands.

Prayer is communication with God, listening and speaking and responding in faith and obedience. Earlier, Abram listened and obeyed, but now we will hear the conversations that took place between God and Abram.

God spoke a beautiful word to Abram's heart, but Abram came back with, basically, "Great, but what about the kid?" Before God answered, Abram offered God a solution to what seemed to be a difficult thing for God to accomplish. Let's listen in on their conversation.

> Abram said, "O Lord God, what will You give me, since I am childless, and the heir of my house is Eliezer of Damascus?"
>
> And Abram said, "Since You have given no offspring to me, one born in my house is my heir."
>
> Then behold, the word of the Lord came to him, saying, "This man will not be your heir; but one who will come forth from your own body, he shall be your heir."
>
> And He took him outside and said, "Now look toward the heavens, and count the stars, if you are able to count them." And He said to him, "So shall your descendants be." Genesis 15:2–5

Wow! God said no to Abram's plan because He had another plan for Abram's life. He made it very clear that Abram's heir would be the fruit of his own body. God's ways and thoughts and plans are always higher than ours (Isa. 55:8–9).

He even called Abram outside. (Today, these would be fighting words!) He called Abram out and told him to count the stars, then promised him that his descendants would be as such.

Then came the test. How did Abram respond? The next verse is a key verse and a monumental point in Abram's life and relationship with God. If he failed this one, he would struggle with life and he would struggle in his progress with God. Here is Abram's response to "so shall your descendants be": "Then he [Abram] believed in the Lord; and He reckoned it to him as righteousness" (15:6).

Abram believed *in* the Lord. That little word *in* lets us know that Abram had complete faith in God, and that he had totally committed himself to God.

To reckon means to put to one's account. If I were to reckon money to your bank account, it would mean that I put money in or gave you a credit. God reckoned righteousness to Abram's life account in heaven. Abram's name was written in the book of life.

Let me ask you a question. In your process of and progress toward sacrificial obedience, have you come to the moment where you confessed faith in the Lord Jesus Christ? Do you believe, in a life-changing way, what God has said to us New Testament believers about Jesus?

Upon believing, have you given your life to Him and asked Him to live in your heart by His Holy Spirit? If so, then your account in Heaven also says "Righteous! Deserving of Eternal Life." Your name is written in the Lamb's Book of Life, and with that there is eternal security.

If not, then please think on these things. What do you believe about Jesus Christ? I want to be completely honest with you and let you know that unless you believe that

Jesus is the Christ, that He is God, you will die in your sins and never know eternal life. You will never know intimacy with God (John 8:24).

My husband says that being saved is like being pregnant. You either are or you are not. The Word of God puts it like this: "However, you are not in the flesh but in the Spirit, if indeed the Spirit of God dwells in you. But if anyone does not have the Spirit of Christ, he does not belong to Him" (Rom. 8:9).

> And the testimony is this, that God has given us eternal life, and this life is in His Son. He who has the Son has the life; he who does not have the Son of God does not have the life. These things I have written to you who believe in the name of the Son of God, so that you may know that you have eternal life. 1 John 5:11–13

Eternal life is found nowhere else but in the Son of God, Jesus Christ. He who does not have the Son of God does not have life.

We have to get this part exactly right if we are going to go on with God. There are no shortcuts here. You must make an A+ on the issue of salvation. The choice is yours. Choose Christ and live now and forever. This will give you an A+. (For more insights on Abraham's prayer life, see Genesis chapters 12–22.)

THE COVENANT

Our friend Abram was growing in faith and obedience by leaps and bounds. Now came the ultimate point in his life as a believer. God established His promise by cutting a covenant with Abram. This is really strange, but watch what happened (Gen. 15:8–21).

God told Abram to gather certain animals and to cut them—with the exception of the birds—letting their blood run and separating them on opposite sides of each other. Stay with me now. God then put Abram into a deep sleep. In the dark of night, God spoke deeply into Abram's heart. He told him that his descendents would be slaves in Egypt for four hundred years. God said that He would then judge Egypt, and that Abram's descendents would come out with many possessions.

This is very important because Abram's descendents would need to be encouraged during their time of slavery. They too would need this promise to keep their hope alive during the hardest period of their lives.

God's presence was known by Abraham and there were no doubts that God Himself established the covenant. God sealed His promise with a blood sacrifice. In the New Covenant in the New Testament, God also sealed His promise by sacrificing His only Son, Jesus Christ.

Think about this for a moment. Have you ever wondered whether or not God is serious about His promises to bless and to redeem? Have you ever questioned the faithfulness of God? I have. But when I come back to the cross and see God's Son hanging there, so that all of God's promises will be yes and amen for me, then I know without a doubt that I can trust God at any and every place along my journey of sacrificial obedience.

Abram knew that God had established this covenant, and he could rest assured that God would be faithful to fulfill His promise. It is time now for you and me to wake up from our spiritual slumber and see what God has done for us. Once we understand the importance of putting our full trust in God's faithful heart and His Word, we are called to "the place that God will show us." Then we will have the spiritual fortitude to climb the mountain and make the sacrifice. We can live a life of sacrificial obedience to God because we know the sovereign Most High God, who is the Giver of Eternal Life.

GROWING IN GRACE

Progress in Abram's life seemed to be much more consistent after the covenant with God. He started out hearing from God occasionally, but then God spoke more frequently, and Abram even asked God some tough questions. God answered and Abram responded. His prayer life grew, as well as his faith in God and his knowledge of God.

I hope that you are encouraged by the process and the progress that you have seen in Abram's life. Seems like in our day, if you are not a spiritual giant then there is no place for you in ministry and in the kingdom of God. I am glad that God is not that way. I am thankful that His ways are higher than our ways and His thoughts than our thoughts.

God really has trained me on the job. I became a Christian when I was seven years old. I lived in a Christian home, so I learned quite a bit about God and what it meant to be a Christian. My mom and dad took great care of me. I always knew that if ever I would need them, they would be there for me.

They were there all through grade school and college, teaching me and watching me grow. After graduating from college, I worked for a few years at Heritage USA, a Christian resort near Charlotte, North Carolina, which was a spiritual eye-opener for me. For the first time in my life I was around people from different parts of the world who had different spiritual experiences than I had. At first, I thought they were all weird, but I came to know that they were just a little further along in the process than I was.

I wanted to experience God like they were experiencing God. I started to pray more and spend more time with "more spiritual people." I learned a little, but there was still a thirst in my soul that was not being quenched.

I left Heritage USA and began to sing with the group TRUTH, where I stayed for six years. Still, there was something within me that was not satisfied. While working with TRUTH, I learned that there were even more people in the world who were not like me. They had very different ideas about God than I had. They also had different experiences with God than I had ever known.

This left me searching. I did not necessarily want what they had, but I did want to know more about the God whom I was claiming to know. I read lots of Christian books and God used those books to begin a growing process in me that continues to this day.

With the help of some dear friends, I left TRUTH and started out in a solo ministry. After about six months on the road as a Christian solo artist, I discovered that my theology was as shallow as a kiddy pool. I loved Jesus. I had received His Spirit. I knew what lots of people thought of Him and I had read lots of books about Him, but I knew that I still did not know Him as I wanted to. I was not in a place where I was about to ask Him some of the questions that Abram asked.

I felt spiritually dry inside, almost to the point of physical pain. I could not stand it and I knew that something had to change. I told a friend how I was feeling and she told me about an inductive Bible study class.

I decided to go. On the first day, the teacher said that we would study the book of Romans for two years! She said that we could write our prayer requests on a sheet of paper because this was not a prayer group. This was a Bible study, and we were there to study the Bible! Then in a nice, sweet voice she said, "Now let's get started." She prayed a short prayer and we began studying the book of Romans.

During her prayer, I was very arrogant in my immature Christian spirit. I told God that I would be the smartest one in the class and that it would not take me two years to study a letter that came in the mail.

I now truly believe that I was the most unlearned person in the class. Eighteen months later, after studying through Romans 12:1–2, I was on my face before a holy God, in total awe of who He was and all that He had done.

Today when I think about a key word in those two verses, *therefore*, I am still on my face. I have learned to look for what the *therefore* is there for. When I realized that *therefore* connected this passage to chapters 1 through 11, I finally began to understand what this verse really meant. I was overwhelmed with the presence of God; and I kid you not, it put me on my face.

Today, that thirst is still there, but it is a different kind of thirst. It is a thirst for righteousness, and for more of a deep relational knowledge of the God who loves me so much. Peter said that grace and peace are multiplied to us through the knowledge of God and of Jesus our Lord. He also said that God's divine power, His Spirit within us, has granted us "everything pertaining to life and godliness, through the true knowledge of Him who called us by His own glory and excellence" (2 Peter 1:2–3).

The word for knowledge in these verses is the Greek word *epinosis*, which means a deep relational knowledge. I love this word, and I love the lesson that is in these two verses.

Peter ended his book by telling the believers to grow in grace. He was encouraging the process. "Grow in the grace and knowledge of our Lord and Savior Jesus Christ" (2 Peter 3:18). The word for knowledge in this verse is the Greek word *gnosis*, which means a learned knowledge.

I believe Peter was saying that as we study God's Word, we grow in the studied knowledge of God through His Word, and our relational knowledge of Him deepens and becomes more intimate. We increase in grace and peace as we experience the deep, thorough, intimate things of God.

Even as I write this book, I am encouraged as I remember my journey of growing in grace and in the *epinosis* and *gnosis* of my Lord, my Savior Jesus Christ. The learning never ends and neither does the intimacy.

EL SHADDAI

Father Abraham was one who grew in grace and in a deep relational knowledge of God. He did not have the Holy Scriptures as we do, but he did have the very presence of God. I will tell you once again: let's do the best we can with what we know to be God's truth and watch God be faithful to complete the work of salvation that He has begun in us.

The first verse of Genesis 17 is my altar verse for this year: "Now when Abram was ninety-nine years old, the Lord appeared to Abram and said to him, 'I am God Almighty; walk before me, and be blameless.'"

Abram had just learned another name for God. God Almighty, *El Shaddai*, meaning "all-sufficient." This is just great: Abram was ninety-nine years old, God had promised him descendents, and there was still no baby! He spoke to Abram and said that He was all-sufficient. He was everything that Abram and Sarai needed to have a baby. Their responsibility was to walk before Him and be blameless.

I love it. *Walk before Me* means "keep up to pace with Me. Don't try to figure this one out. Don't manipulate My words. Don't worry about what you think should be happening months or years from now. Just walk with Me today. I am everything you need today and tomorrow. I have spoken and I will bring it to pass."

> "I will establish My covenant between Me and you, and I will multiply you exceedingly." Genesis 17:2

Who will do the establishing? God will. I think Abram and Sarai only heard that they were going to have descendents, because if they had heard with their hearts that God would establish His covenant with them, then perhaps they would not have made some of the mistakes that they made. I will talk more about that in just a minute. For now, let's look again at Genesis 17:1–2 and receive these verses into our hearts.

We all have issues that only God can resolve. He makes us all a great promise in these two verses. He is the all-sufficient God and He will establish His covenant between Himself and us. Our responsibility—and don't miss this—is to walk with Him daily and be blameless.

Blameless means complete, whole, or sound. How do we do this? We do this by looking into the Word of God and living by its counsel. Remember our discussion on Joshua 1:8 in chapter 2? Ditto!

God says, "I will multiply you exceedingly." I really believe this. I have seen this in my life and ministry—so much so that I cannot rely on anyone or anything to "multiply" me except the Lord God, El Shaddai.

Almost every time that I am out sharing in ministry, someone will ask me that famous question, "How do I get started in ministry?" My heart sinks because I know that when I tell them my story they are going to walk away and be disappointed. It makes me think of the rich young ruler who wanted to follow Jesus. Jesus counseled him to sell everything he had, give his money to the poor, and then follow Jesus. Jesus said this to him because money and riches were his god. In a relationship with Christ, we are to have no other gods. The young man walked away, and we never see him again in Scripture (Matt. 19:21–22).

The answer to the question is, "I don't know!" I don't know what Jesus will say to you to get you started in a full-time ministry. But I do know that if you will walk before Him and be blameless, He will establish His covenant with you and will multiply you exceedingly.

Every album I have ever recorded was offered to me by someone whose heart had been moved upon by the Spirit of God. I write books because God has moved on the heart of my publisher. No lie. I was at home just doing what ladies do when they are at home alone! I opened the mail and there was a letter asking if I would be interested in writing a book. That really is how it happened.

I sing concerts and speak at conferences because God moves on someone's heart, as well as my own. God has been faithful to work out His plans in my life and I have not had to try to manipulate any circumstances to make things happen. It was all offered because God moved on the hearts of His people, and I just said, "Yes, Lord."

Even the people who work in our scheduling office are there because God moved on their hearts. I have no rich and famous relatives pulling strings for me. I don't even have a lot of friends in "high places" doing favors for me. (Watch out for the high places—there is idolatry in high places.)

I was one of those who had no clue about the prayer of Jabez until Mr. Bruce Wilkinson wrote his book. I read it in response to all that was going on in my life and found that God had done for me what He did for Jabez. I prayed the prayer as a praise, and thanked God for what He has done.

The prayer that I pray for my life and ministry is a prayer that includes the prayer of Jabez. It is the prayer of the Lord Jesus Christ: "Thy kingdom come; Thy will be done."

As a matter of fact, ministry is very hard work. Good and evil travel on the same road and get to the same place at just about the same time. So with the good and glorious come the ugly and the evil.

But I am without excuse. I know the road that I am to take, and any other way for me would be sin. I know that God is El Shaddai. I am to walk before Him and be blameless. I am to fully believe that He will establish His covenant between Himself and me, and that He is the one who multiplies me exceedingly.

This year we are in need of one more staff person. I am waiting for God to move on that person's heart and on my heart so that he or she will join us in ministry and not be here with another agenda. I know that God will do it. He has promised, and His Word stands.

Walk before Him and be blameless. He will establish His covenant. He will not only add to your life, He will multiply you exceedingly! He promised this to Abraham and I believe He wants to do this in our lives. Thus saith the Lord.

ON YOUR FACE

God spoke these words to Abram, and I want you to see Abram's response: "Abram fell on his face, and God talked with him" (Gen. 17:3).

Abram fell on his face and God talked with him. This is true worship. This is the posture and the position of true worship: we fall on our faces before a holy God. Applied daily, this is the posture of the heart, bowed down to Almighty God, yielded to the Word of the Lord, living in the strength of the Holy Spirit and under His control.

Note that God talked with Abram. Abram was not asleep and he was not passed out. He was not old and crippled. He had not fallen and couldn't get up. He was a worshiper! He got on his face in the presence of a holy God, and God talked with him.

Check this out: this is the first time the Scriptures say that God talked with Abram. He had progressed in his relationship with God, and he was experiencing God in a whole new way. This was deeper. This was sweeter.

I know this moment. This reminds me of the day I got on my face to acknowledge God as Adonai, and I chose to let Him be Lord and Master over cancer in my life. That day, God talked with me and gave me peace in my soul and a song like no other.

The day "I got picked," God's presence came. He did not talk, but His presence was enough. El Shaddai was more than enough!

Are you longing for God to talk with you? He wants to because He loves you so much. Worship Him. Worship Him biblically and not denominationally. Let go of all that you think you know about Him. Get on your face. Stay there until He talks with you. Draw near to God and He will draw near to you (James 4:8)

FAITHFUL TO COMPLETE IT

He who has begun the good work of salvation in you will be faithful to complete it. That is God's word to us in Philipppians 1:6. The work of salvation begins when we receive the Spirit of God into our hearts through faith in the Lord Jesus Christ, and it continues until we put on immortality. This is what we have seen in the life of Abram, and this is what is happening in the life of every true believer.

After revealing himself as El Shaddai, God completed establishing the Abrahamic covenant. He changed Abram's name to "Abraham," and Sarai to "Sarah." Their new identity was now in the God that they served and not in the god of their fathers (Gen. 17).

God also gave them the sign of the covenant—circumcision for Abraham at ninety-nine years old and for Ishmael at thirteen. He also circumcised every male in his household. The covenant was two-fold. There was the promise of a seed and the promise of land. The seed was Christ (Gal. 3:16). God promised to provide a land for His people. God gave Christ so that we could know the intimate relationship with God that we have discussed in this book. God was faithful to all those who put their faith and trust in Him to experience His promises.

His Word is complete; His Word stands. If He has begun this good work in you, you can know that He will be faithful to complete it. Your final report, with God in charge of your life, will yield an A+.

Chapter Six

Passion of Sacrifice

*P*assion! Intense emotional excitement. These emotions can be good or bad, but in every case they are intense and exciting.

We girls have no problem understanding this at all. We are probably God's most passionate creatures. Women have more emotion than any other creature I have ever seen. We are passionate about almost everything. From our shoes to our hair and nails, to our clothes, our homes, our children's clothes, husband's clothes, to social status . . . did I say clothes?

This list goes on and on. We are passionate about more things than we probably care to admit. I really don't think that we can help it most of the time. I am not a psychologist, neither do I have any formal learning on the "science" of the female gender, but I have lived as a female all of my life—some forty years!—so I know that *we care*, and we care a whole lot!

At least I do. I care about everything. My husband (bless him, Lord) is always saying to me, "That is none of your business. Stay out of it. Their problem is not your problem." I know, but I can't help it. I don't care if it's a deep need or a fun party. I care about what is going on and feel like my presence could make any situation better. What a hoot!

Call it "sensitive." I am thankful that we girls are sensitive. I believe sensitivity separates us Christians from the rest of the world. The world is very insensitive, competitive, dog-eat-dog, and matter of fact. Of course you will find a lot of this in Christendom as well, I'm sorry to say.

But as a rule, the Christian heart is a sensitive heart and is very caring about more things than a heart that does not have the Spirit of God.

Whereas I wholeheartedly believe that Holy Scripture is absolute truth, I also know that His Spirit of love and grace keeps the hatchet from falling on our heads when we fall short of His absolutes. Yes, right is right and wrong is wrong. Right and wrong are determined by God's Word. There is total authority in God's Word, and when His Word is violated, I am passionate about it. When God's Words are honored, I am passionate about it. When His truths are looked upon apathetically, I care, and I want to see apathy turned into passion.

NEVER INDIFFERENT

A few months ago I was working with Bruce Marchiano. Bruce played the part of Jesus in the Visual Bible's video production of the book of Matthew. We were together for an entire weekend, so I got to hear him talk a lot about what it was like to play the role of Jesus. He also spoke about some of the historical and biblical facts that impacted the life of Jesus. These things seemed to humble his heart, and often he would say something like, "I hope I played that part right."

Talking about the filming of the crucifixion, Bruce told us that he had gotten beat-up pretty bad in rehearsal before filming the scene, so most of his bruises were real. The guys whose job it was to beat him up may have done their job a little too well. He said that before he even got to the set, the preparation had made him very tired, almost to the point of exhaustion. Nevertheless, he wanted to play the part right.

After make-up and wardrobe, Bruce was ready to call it a day and go home, but the time had come for them to film the sufferings of Christ and the crucifixion. As he talked about all of this, I got to watch footage of the scenes. I could see that he was not just acting, he was really hurting. I tried to watch the film as if it were just a movie in which Bruce was just acting, but the Spirit of the Lord would not let go of my emotions.

Bruce told us about the physical challenge of acting out the trial and the scourging. He talked about how the director stayed very close to him and kept asking if he was all right. Bruce would keep saying yes, even though he was hurting.

They finally got to the crucifixion scene, and Bruce was up on the cross. While he was bruised and his make-up was heavier than he'd expected, he knew his discomfort did not compare to the "make-up" Christ wore that day. The director was on a scaffold beside him calling out to him, "Bruce, are you okay?" Bruce just nodded his head as they continued to shoot the scene.

While they were filming the crucifixion, the blood make-up from Bruce's head began to drip to his face. The director called out, "The blood, the blood! There it is! Look at the blood! That was for you and me. Make sure you get the blood!"

This went on for quite a while. One last time, the director called out to him, "Bruce, are you all right?" Bruce turned his head toward the director, hardly able to nod, but managing enough to let him know that he was willing to do it again. Bruce said that when the director saw his eyes, he did not see an actor playing a role, but a man dying, and he cut the scene. "It's a wrap!"

While we listened to Bruce tell his story, our hearts were stirred as the Spirit of God moved upon us. Even now, it is not easy to tell the story without being over-whelmed at the reality of what happened for us some two thousand years ago. God did not cut the scene, but saw a man dying and let him die—for you and for me.

My heart hurt for Bruce as a person because the price he had to pay to play the role seemed very high. Then God reminded me that His Son Jesus paid the supreme price, His blood—real blood—for my life.

Then I heard God saying to me, "Indifferent! That is one emotion that I have never felt. I am not indifferent! I care about everyone and everything."

I told this to Bruce at the end of the meeting. He said that indifference was probably the one emotion he never felt as he played the role of Jesus. He said that Jesus was passionate about everything. Absolutely everything!

He cared about a family that was about to be humili-ated at a wedding because the wine had run out (John 2:1–10). Imagine that!

He cared so much for His Father's temple that He made a scourge and cleansed the moneychangers out of it (John 2:14–17).

He cared about Nicodemus enough to stay up late one night and explain to him that, though he was a religious leader in Israel, he—like everyone else—must be born again (John 3:1–21).

He cared about that woman at the well so much so that He passed through Samaria to bring to her Living Water. She declared to others that He knew everything she had ever done (John 4:4–29).

Jesus, being a Jew, but also being God, cared about the Samaritans, who were considered as dogs by the Jews, and brought the good news of the gospel to them (John 4:39–42).

He cared about a government official and his sick son enough that He sent His word and healed the boy (John 4:49–53).

He cared about a man who had been sick for thirty-eight years. He told him to take up his pallet and walk and the man did just that (John 5:5–9).

He cared so much about His Father's will that He did nothing on His own initiative (John 5:30).

He cared about a group of fisherman, caught in a storm out at sea. He walked on the water and brought them to safety (John 6:16–21).

He cared about hunger and weariness, so He miraculously fed a multitude with two fish and five loaves of bread (John 6:1–13).

He cared about the choices and the "thirst" of His children and offered us the living water of His Spirit (John 7:37–39).

He cared about a woman caught in adultery. He got rid of her accusers, did not condemn her, and told her to sin no more (John 8:1–11).

He cared about truth, so He spoke it without compromise, knowing that it would set us free from sin and death (John 8:11–59).

He cares about physical and spiritual blindness and offers Himself, the Light of the world (John 9:5–7).

He cares about His flock, knowing that we are sheep who need Him as a Shepherd (John 10:1–16).

He cares when we hurt and He weeps with us (John 11:33–35).

He cares that we get the bigger vision so He allows us to suffer and even die, because He is the resurrection and the life (John 11:25, 40).

He cares about intimacy with us, so He lets us anoint Him with our worship (John 12:3).

He cares about the destiny of those who will not receive Him, and He wails for them (Luke 19:41).

He cares that we serve each other so He showed us how by becoming the Chief Servant (John 13:3–16).

He cares that your heart is troubled, and freely gives you His peace (John 14:27).

He cares that we might drift away and tells us to abide (John 15:1–15).

He cares that we are weak and sends His Spirit to empower us (John 16:5–15).

He cares about us in a world that hates us, so He prays for us (John 17).

He cares about our debt to sin, so He suffered and died for us (John 18, 19). This is the *passion* of Jesus Christ!

So that our debt to sin would be paid in full, He conquered death and rose victoriously from the dead (John 20).

He cares that we are afraid, so He will walk through the locked doors and walls that we build in order to bring us the comfort of His presence (John 20:19).

He cares that we have "living proof" of our great salvation, so He rose from the dead and showed himself to over 500 witnesses.

He cares that we still might not believe, so He keeps coming to us, commissioning us to feed His sheep and to follow Him (John 21).

Indifferent? Never! He cares about us. He cares about everything. Nothing escapes Him. He sees all, knows all, and He cares about all.

"Does He care about my . . . ?"

"Yes!"

"What about my . . . ?"

"Yes!"

"Then why doesn't He fix it?"

"Why don't you give it to Him, and stop trying to fix it yourself? If you give it to Him, He will take it. If you are not going to give it to Him, then stop complaining!"

Indifferent? Never! He cares about it all.

LOVE IS THE FACTOR

What is the motivation behind the caring heart of the Lord Jesus? Why is He so passionate about everything? Great questions with an easy answer. Love is the factor. The love of God is what makes Him so passionate about everything.

The love of God is like faith in God, or the fear of God, in that it demands a response. Love is an action, and because God loves so deeply, He is filled with passion, and is always responding to us in love. The love of God causes Him to care about the intimate details of our lives, and He is ever working things together for our good.

Jesus loves us so much that, as our Eternal High Priest, He ever lives to intercede for us. He is always praying for us because He loves us so much (Heb. 7:25).

> God so loved the world, that He gave His only begotten Son, that whoever believes in Him shall not perish, but have eternal life. John 3:16

> God demonstrates His own love toward us, in that while we were yet sinners, Christ died for us. Romans 5:8

I always enjoy Bible teachers or preachers who are filled with passion when they speak. You can see that they love God and His Word with all of their being. This encourages me to love God more and to seek to know Him better through His Word.

Look at what the Word of God says about God's love in us.

> The love of God has been poured out within our hearts through the Holy Spirit who was given to us. Romans 5:5
>
> For I am convinced that neither death, nor life, nor angels, nor principalities, nor things present, nor things to come, nor powers, nor height, nor depth, nor any other created thing, will be able to separate us from the love of God, which is in Christ Jesus our Lord. Romans 8:38–39
>
> For this is the love of God, that we keep His commandments; and His commandments are not burdensome. 1 John 5:3

Without a doubt, the love of God in us will create passion for the things of God and cause us to live differently. We will be sensitive and we will care a lot. Keep yourselves in the love of God.

THE PASSION OF JESUS CHRIST

God does love us and He does care about every detail of our lives. He cares so much about our sin that He sent His Son Jesus to suffer and die for us.

The definitions of *passion* that I gave at the beginning of this chapter are actually the second and third definitions listed in Webster's dictionary. The first definition of passion is "the sufferings of Jesus on the cross or after the last supper." That absolutely blew my mind. There I was, reading a dictionary, and the first thing it said to me about passion was that the term is related to the life of my Savior, Jesus Christ.

I had to find this in the Word of God. It was not hard at all.

To these He also presented Himself alive after His suffering, by many convincing proofs, appearing to them over a
period of forty days and speaking of the things concerning
the kingdom of God. Acts 1:3

The word *suffering* in this verse is translated from the
Greek word *pascho*, which means to experience a sensation
or impression, usually painful, though it can be used in a
good sense.

These sensations are called passion. The deep feelings
of pain and suffering that our Lord Jesus underwent when
He was arrested and crucified are called the *passion* of Jesus
Christ.

He felt the horrible sensation of the scourging on His
back. He felt the spittle in His face and the plucking out of
His beard. He felt the thorns bearing down on His fore-
head and blood and sweat dripping into His weary eyes
and opened flesh. He felt the sting of the splinters of the
wooden cross on His back and its heaviness on His shoulders. Yet nothing was more heavy and painful than our sin,
which He now bore *in* His body.

He felt the nails in His wrists and His feet. He felt sepa-
ration from the Father. He felt death. Our death.

You want to talk about passion. That's passion! He
didn't just die, He suffered and died. He suffered from
"Let this cup pass," to "I thirst" and "It is finished." He
said "Yes" to passion and pain, "Yes" to sacrifice.

He loved His Father and had come to do His will. The
wages of our sin is death; Jesus' death, if we believe. The
Father ordained it and allowed it because He loves us too
much to let us perish without offering us hope.

We see in Jesus deep emotion, pain, and suffering—the
Passion of Sacrifice, worship at its finest hour, all compelled
by the deep, rich, and incomprehensible love of God.

FOR THE JOY

There are Christians all over the world who suffer for the cause of Christ more than you and I may ever know. But we need to know that the day and time will come when we are called to the passion of sacrifice.

God will prepare you for suffering. He will prepare you for emotions and pain that you have never felt before. The process and progress of growing in faith and obedience will prepare you for those moments. If you are willing to go the distance, play the part right, build altars along the way, and make the sacrifice that He has asked of you, you will be equipped for suffering when it comes your way.

If you are at this tender yet tough moment in your life right now, then know that His Spirit in you will empower you to endure, to make right choices, to play the part right, and bring glory to the Father. Know also that if you are there, God knows that you are spiritually strong enough to be there, and that strength is the love of God, which He has poured into your heart by the Holy Spirit whom He has given you. At just the right time God, the sovereign director of your life and mine, will call out, "Cut the scene," and you will hear Him say, "Well done."

Rest will follow. Rest on earth or rest in His holy presence. No more bloody garments. You will wear a white robe of righteousness. You will enjoy an intimate meal with the Director, who loves you, who was there for you and is pleased with the perfecting of your faith.

Sacrificial obedience leads to intimacy with God. So hold nothing back. Give it all you've got because you have got a lot. Finish strong. Fix your eyes on Jesus, the author and finisher of your faith—who, *for the joy* set before Him endured the cross, endured the passion, despising its shame, and is now intimately seated at the right hand of the throne of God.

Chapter Seven

People and Sacrifice

I once heard the president of a rather large company say to his employees that life would be so much easier if we did not have to deal with people. Most of our problems have to do with issues we have with other people. If we just did not have to deal with people, life would be a lot easier.

Of course, he went on to say, there is a down side to not having people around as well. Without people, life would be meaningless. There would be no families, no church, no parties, no sports! And what is life without baseball?

We girls would have no one around to tell how to live their lives. And what would we do if we couldn't give our opinion and advice to everyone, whether they ask for it or not? What would I do without my friend Shanda, who listens to me rattle on and on because I have had such a yucky day?

Now I know that there are some people we would rather do without, but for the most part, we love and need people. We would be miserable without each other. Just try to imagine a life with no other people. Who would turn on your computer or change the tape in your VCR? (Just joking.)

We may not always realize it, but we rely on each other quite a bit. Life would be very different and difficult without the people we interact with every day.

I have a friend who has a little boy who spends lots of time with his mom and dad, his grandma and grandpa, and his nanny. His parents are in full-time ministry, so he is around a lot of people a lot of the time.

Just recently both his grandparents went to be with the Lord, and for a while his nanny was not with him. His parents were on a break from traveling, so just the three of them were at home together. He climbed into bed one night and started crying. His mom and dad went to check on him, asking what was the matter. He said, "I have no people." Of course, they consoled him and climbed into bed with him. Once again his life was filled with people.

Life just was not the same without his "people," and life for you and me is not as much fun without our people. The fact of the matter is, we are going to have people in our lives forever, so we would do well to learn how to deal with people now.

Abraham would have had an easier life if he had not had to deal with the people around him. However, I do not think he would have known God as he did had those folks not brought into his life the challenges that they did. The truth is they were like you and me—human. They had opinions and ideas, and they shared them with Abraham. Sometimes they were good ideas and sometimes not, but Abraham learned when and how to listen to people and when and how to listen to God.

I like people. I am a people-person for the most part. But as with anything, we have to learn how to deal wisely with people.

This chapter will be just a little "girlfriend talk" about people. Sound good? Then get some tea and a two-point energy bar, and let's talk.

SARAH

We meet Sarah first as Sarai. She was Abram's half-sister, daughter of his father, and also Abram's wife. She played the role of sister a few times, but her main role was wife.

We know quite a bit about Sarah, and I like her. I believe I understand how and why she thought the way she did. Good or bad, this lady was involved in her husband's life, and I truly believe that she did all she could to make the most of her life and her husband's. First Peter 3:6 says that she obeyed Abraham and called him "lord." (Thanks a lot, Sarah!)

I believe that Abraham shared with her what God told him, and that she did everything she could to see to it that Abraham stayed on track. She was not fussy when he said, "Honey, we're moving." She just packed the tent and moved with him.

I hope you're hearing me, girls. I know of several men who are miserable and know that they are out of the will of God because they are trying to please a wife who does not care about the will of God for her husband. She wants to live with her family or her friends, while her husband and children accommodate her, and thus live short of what God has planned for their family.

Girls, our husbands have been given a lot of responsibility toward us from God. If you have a man like Abraham and he is doing all he can to follow the will of God for his life and the life of his family, trust the Spirit of God to lead him. Follow in full support. Obey him and call him "lord" (with a lower-case "l" of course). My lord!

Open communication is the key. Talk about what God has put on both your hearts. I believe that if you are both honest, you will be able to discern the will of God.

Pray for your husband and pray with him. God reveals Himself when we pray. Maintain an open heart to the Spirit of the Lord. There will be a unity and a oneness that will strengthen you from one event to the next.

Never try to make God's will happen. Sarah tried this with Hagar, and the world is a mess today because of it.

Yet God allowed it. Isn't that how we ladies sometimes are? We are going to help God all we can. But learn this lesson: never try to manipulate the will of God. (Please read the full story in Genesis 16!)

Have you seen the little flyer that says, "Good morning! This is God, and I have a wonderful plan for your life today, and I don't need your help!" Not only is God all-sufficient, He is self-sufficient. He has contained within Himself all that He needs.

Then why did He create us? Because God is love, and love wants an object for its affection. God created us to pour out His love on us, to be our God, and for us to be His people. That is pretty cool.

But He really does not need our help. We just need to seek to know His will, which we know through the Bible, and submit ourselves to it. God watches over His Word. Do you know why? He watches over His Word to perform it. Let God perform His will in your life and in the life of your husband and the people around you.

Wanting to be helpful is not a bad thing. We just need to be led by the Spirit of God and not by our own emotions and passions.

If you feel like you have heard from God and that you have a word of encouragement for someone, then humbly share your heart with him or her. Do the same for your husband. If he is like Abraham, seeking after the heart of God and desiring to hear from Him, then he will warmly receive your gentle word. If for one reason or another your husband is one who is disobedient to the Word of God, we have instructions in First Peter (see verses below) that help us know how we can make life better for him and others around him.

I believe that if we make these verses our prayer for ourselves, and stop looking for a verse for our husbands and the people we deal with daily, then we will see God bring about the change in our "people" that may truly need to happen. But change is something that only God can bring.

> For you have been called for this purpose, since Christ also suffered for you, leaving you an example for you to follow in His steps, who committed no sin, nor was any deceit found in His mouth; and while being reviled, He did not revile in return; while suffering, He uttered no threats, but kept entrusting Himself to Him who judges righteously; and He Himself bore our sins in His body on the cross, so that we might die to sin and live to righteousness; for by His wounds you were healed.
>
> For you were continually straying like sheep, but now you have returned to the Shepherd and Guardian of your souls.
>
> In the same way, you wives, be submissive to your own husbands so that even if any of them are disobedient to the word, they may be won without a word by the behavior of their wives, as they observe your chaste and respectful behavior.
>
> Your adornment must not be merely external—braiding the hair, and wearing gold jewelry, or putting on dresses; but let it be the hidden person of the heart, with the imperishable quality of a gentle and quiet spirit, which is precious in the sight of God.
>
> For in this way in former times the holy women also, who hoped in God, used to adorn themselves, being submissive to their own husbands, just as Sarah obeyed Abraham, calling him lord, and you have become her children if you do what is right without being frightened by any fear. 1 Peter 2:21–3:6

Trust the Spirit of the Lord in your life, in your husband's life, and in the lives of your "people." You live biblically. You live sacrificially. God will be faithful to bring you pleasure and intimacy with your family, your friends, and with Himself. He did it for Sarah. He will do it for you.

HAGAR: SINGLE AND PREGNANT

Precious Hagar was totally caught in the middle of Abraham and Sarah's mess. Hagar was Sarah's Egyptian maidservant, whom Sarah gave to Abraham that she might bear him a son, an heir to the promise of God. Oh, Sarah. I know that this was a common practice in those days, but I have never known this scenario to be a good one. It's hard enough for a woman to live under one roof with herself, how much harder it would be to live with the younger, fertile mother of your husband's baby. That was a disaster fixin' to happen!

Hagar was a servant, carrying the child of her master, who was not in love with her. She was a puppet to them. Nevertheless, just like a woman, when her pregnancy began to show, she flaunted it in front of Sarah, and of course this made Sarah very angry. Check this out: Sarah blamed Abraham! (Gen. 16:5)

Abraham reminded Sarah that this girl was under her care and that she had the power to do to her whatever she wanted. (Don't tell a woman that!) So Sarah treated Hagar harshly, and Hagar ran away.

Sounds like a soap opera, doesn't it?

So there was Hagar—single, pregnant, homeless, without food or water, and with no people. She was suffering the unfair consequences of what had happened to her. The angel of the Lord appeared to her in the "desert of her days." Hagar told the angel her story, the unedited version. And get this: the angel told her to return to Sarah and submit to her. That must have been a tough word to hear from the Lord.

He told her that He would greatly multiply her descendants so that they would be too many to count (16:10). He also told her that she was carrying a son, and that she was to name him Ishmael because the Lord had given heed and had heard and seen her affliction (16:11).

God showed compassion to Hagar. God will show compassion to you and to me. God cares for you and for your children. He has a great plan and purpose for your life. Even if you are in your darkest hour, He will be there for you. Listen for His voice, and do "whatever He says to you" (John 2:5).

God's comfort to Hagar is like that of a husband. Isaiah 54:5–7 tells us that the Lord will be a husband to His people.

> "For your husband is your Maker, whose name is the Lord of hosts; and your Redeemer is the Holy One of Israel, who is called the God of all the earth. For the Lord has called you, like a wife forsaken and grieved in spirit, even like a wife of one's youth when she is rejected," says your God. "For a brief moment I forsook you, but with great compassion I will gather you." Isaiah 54:5–7

I am an author, and it seems I am supposed to have great spiritual analysis when I present scriptural truth to you. The truth is, I don't always understand everything God says in His Word, and I would be leery of anyone who always thinks he or she does. I have several questions about God's dealings with Hagar and Ishmael. It seems that neither one of them was deserving of the life they came to know. As far as I can see, Hagar simply obeyed Sarah, and Ishmael was the product of that obedience.

God told Hagar that her son, whom He would bless, would be a wild donkey of a man, and that his hand would be against everyone, and everyone's hand would be against him. God said that he would not be the heir to Abraham's promise, for this child would live east of all his brothers (Gen. 16:12).

Still today, this is what the fighting in the Middle East is all about: Ishmael and Isaac. I remember being in Israel, on the steps of the Temple Mount, where we were studying this story. We were told to be very quiet there, and not to start anything that would look like a riot.

Well, the teacher kept asking us questions as she taught, and our answers began to sound like a chant that could start a riot. She asked who would receive the promises given to Abraham. All three hundred of us answered, Abraham, Isaac, and Jacob . . . just as the Muslim leaders of the temple were walking by. I just knew we were all going to be dead. As it was, they were not sure just what was happening, so they did not jump to conclusions. They went on their way. Thank you, Jesus!

Back to Hagar. She humbled herself before the God of Abraham, and her obedient response afforded her a very intimate moment with God. In Genesis 16:13, from the story of Hagar, we get one of the names of God: *Jehovah Roi*, the God who sees. "Then she called the name of the Lord who spoke to her, 'You are a God who sees'; for she said, 'Have I even remained alive here after seeing Him?'"

God saw this single woman all alone in the desert, and He came to her, revealed Himself to her, and instructed her on what she was to do next. She obeyed God and went back to Abraham and Sarah. They received her and she gave birth to a son, Ishmael, whose life was exactly what God said it would be. My heart goes out to Hagar, the bondwoman.

Children should come into our lives at God's timing and in God's way. You will have to discern in your spirit God's plan for you in regard to children. Even greater than that, we are to receive the will of God in God's time and in God's way. He never asks for help—just for cooperation. We have to be faithful to hear Him and obey Him, maintaining a heart for God in every area of our lives.

Remember from our chapter on passion that God cares about everything and is indifferent about nothing. It does matter how we live! When we sow to the flesh we reap the flesh, which is opposed to the Spirit; but when we sow to the Spirit we reap that which is eternal.

I hope that Hagar did not fall in love with the idea of having any kind of relationship with Abraham. We girls want a commitment after a little kiss on the lips. Can you imagine what must have been in Hagar's mind after being with Abraham and discovering that she was carrying his son? Whoa, that's deep. There was no way around this. Her heart was going to get broken. Being in love with love always gets us into trouble, and the only way out is to fall in love with Jesus, and let Him be a husband to us all the days of our lives.

Once when I was single and traveling alone in Atlanta, Georgia, I decided to have lunch with Jesus. I hate eating alone, but all of my friends in Atlanta were working that day. I decided to eat a chicken sandwich at a free-standing Chick-fil-A in Marietta and to "have a little talk with Jesus." I sat down and asked Him a question that I really didn't care if He answered or not. I asked about my husband.

I even got a little spiritual. I told Him that I know that my Maker is my husband, yada, yada, yada, but I knew deep within my heart that one day I would be married. I didn't really want to get married right away. I was a very content to be single, but I just felt that marriage was in my future.

I knew that God knows everything, so I thought I would ask a silly but direct question, just to see what He would say. I asked Him to just give me my husband's name. I told God that surely he was in Atlanta. There were lots of wonderful men in Atlanta, and if He would just give me his name, I would look for it in the big, giant, Atlanta phone directory and give him a call.

I was being silly and just trying to have a good lunch all by myself. Well, the Lord honored my lunch invitation, and no sooner was I was done being silly then He clearly said, "What is the rest of that verse? You know, the one that says your Maker is your husband."

I thought, what does it say? Oh, yeah! Your Maker is your husband, the Lord Almighty is His name! I laughed and I laughed until I cried. What a sweet intimate moment with Jesus. I was completely satisfied with that, and I will never forget the joy of that moment with Him. It was like He came all the way from Heaven just to tell me that. What a trip. I will never forget it. His speaking that into my soul changed my life that day.

Now I am married, and my Maker is still my husband. Richard is so glad. The Lord is still the one I look to, to provide all that I need. He is faithful; He is a great husband.

Jehovah Roi is the God who sees you! He sees and knows whether you are single, alone and in trouble, or you just feel that way because you have no "people" around who understand what you are going through. He sees you, hears you, and will come to you. When He speaks, obey and enjoy intimacy with a husband who knows you better than you know yourself, and loves you so very, very much.

BLESS MY MISTAKE

There is reason to believe that Hagar may not have told Abraham about her encounter in the desert with the Lord, because thirteen years after Ishmael was born, God clearly told Abraham and Sarah that they were going to have a baby together, and that it was going to happen in the next year! So for thirteen years Abraham may have been thinking that Ishmael was the son who would receive the promise. God waited thirteen years to clarify what He meant by "heir." Look at the conversation from Genesis 17:16–18: "[God said] 'I will bless her [Sarah], and indeed I will give you a son by her. Then I will bless her, and she shall be a mother of nations; kings of peoples will come from her.' Then Abraham fell on his face and laughed (*I would have, too!*), and said in his heart (*in his heart, but not out loud. He's learning!*), 'Will a child be born to a man one hundred years old? And will Sarah, who is ninety years old, bear a child?' And Abraham said to God, 'Oh that Ishmael might live before You!'"

Five times in one verse God says that the heir will come from Sarah. Thirteen years later! I don't get that, but His ways are higher than my ways.

Abraham now realized that his encounter with Hagar was not the will of God and that his being with her had been a mistake. Abraham asked God to bless his mistake—to bless Ishmael and let him be the heir.

Remember the beginning of this chapter? God told Abraham that He was the all-sufficient God who was more than enough for him. They didn't have the resources within themselves to have a baby, but God would be their Resource. He is El Shaddai.

He even gave him a sign of the covenant that would be established between the two of them. Finally God told him that the heir would come from Sarah. God is God, and He knew when to reveal His plans. His ways are sometimes incomprehensible, nevertheless we are to simply yield to Him.

Abraham and Sarah both laughed. "Will a child be born to a man one hundred years old? And will Sarah, who is ninety years old, bear a child? . . . Oh that Ishmael might live before You."

But God's answer was "no!" His covenant would be established with Isaac, whom Sarah would bear to him at this season of the following year.

God knows who, God knows when, God knows how. I cannot tell you how imperative it is that we hear from God on the issue of having children. I know how desperate some of you are to have children, and your desire may be a God-given desire. But I encourage you to make sure that it is. Children outside of the will of God can cause problems for a lifetime and be "wild donkeys" in our lives. Of course, children are very unpredictable, which is all the more reason we should do everything we can to give them a healthy, godly start and heritage in life.

Now let me clarify. Ishmael was not the mistake. Children are not mistakes, because God is the sovereign giver of life. Abraham's mistake was that he went to Hagar.

I know that he did not have a lot of information from God when that happened, but as they say, hindsight is 20/20. We are blessed with history and the Word of God and the Spirit of God. If God has promised, then we must make it His job to fulfill His promise. You stay out of it, except to trust Him and wait for His orders.

ISHMAEL

The name Ishmael means "God hears," and God did hear Ishmael when he was almost at the point of death (Gen. 21:17). Ishmael was the oldest son of Abraham, and Hagar, the Egyptian maidservant, was his mother. We don't know whether or not Hagar told Ishmael that he was not the heir to his father's promise from God. Maybe she was hoping that she had heard wrong and that her baby would be heir to the promise. Nevertheless, God made it very clear that Sarah's baby, Isaac, would be the heir.

Isaac was born the next year and was weaned three years later. At the weaning celebration, Sarah saw Ishmael mocking Isaac. She told Abraham to drive out Hagar and Ishmael, because Ishmael was not to be an heir with Isaac.

The hostility between Sarah and Hagar, Ishmael and Isaac distressed Abraham because he loved his son Ishmael. Nevertheless, God told Abraham to do as Sarah had said. Then God comforted Abraham and promised to make a nation of Ishmael as well. I was just glad to see a man love his child and want to do right by him, regardless.

> But God said to Abraham, "Do not be distressed because of the lad and your maid; whatever Sarah tells you, listen to her, for through Isaac your descendants shall be named.
>
> "And of the son of the maid I will make a nation also, because he is your descendant."
>
> So Abraham rose early in the morning and took bread and a skin of water and gave them to Hagar, putting them on her shoulder, and gave her the boy, and sent her away. And she departed and wandered about in the wilderness of Beersheba. Genesis 21:12–14

I know that God is sovereign and that His plans and purposes stand, but this breaks my heart. Here was a teenage boy, being given to his mother and then being sent away with nothing but bread and a skin of water. Abraham could have given them a few animals, don't you think? Nevertheless, we can't rewrite Scripture.

The water ran out, and there they were again, alone in the desert. This time Ishmael is not in his mother's womb, but is left to die underneath the shade of a tree.

His mother sat opposite him, but far enough away that she would not see him die. Hagar lifted up her voice and wept. She didn't just cry, she wailed and moaned. Ishmael did the same. He did not just whimper remorsefully over what had happened to him. He was a teenager, and the reality of this moment was absolutely overwhelming. This was bad and it hurt deeply. They had not asked for any of this. Now they were left to die.

But remember the name Ishmael: God hears.

> God heard the lad crying; and the angel of God called to Hagar from heaven and said to her, "What is the matter with you, Hagar? Do not fear, for God has heard the voice of the lad where he is.
>
> "Arise, lift up the lad, and hold him by the hand, for I will make a great nation of him."
>
> Then God opened her eyes and she saw a well of water; and she went and filled the skin with water and gave the lad a drink.
>
> God was with the lad, and he grew; and he lived in the wilderness and became an archer.
>
> He lived in the wilderness of Paran, and his mother took a wife for him from the land of Egypt. Genesis 21:17–21

Ishmael and Hagar lived, but they lived just as God said they would. "He will be a wild donkey of a man, his hand will be against everyone, and everyone's hand will be against him; and he will live to the east of all his brothers" (Gen. 16:12).

Can I be honest with you for a moment? I have struggled with this story. I have questioned God's sovereignty and His timing in all of this. I have hurt for Hagar and Ishmael because they seemed so innocent in all of this.

"Why did You let the encounter with Hagar happen?" I ask God. "Why didn't You stop Abraham? Why would You let a baby boy be born from this union if You knew he was not going to be the heir? Why would you tell Abraham to send them away? Yes, maybe their hearts were not very receptive of Isaac, but You, God, You could have helped their hearts. Why this story? Why did You write this story?"

Today, for me, has been another day of intimacy with a holy God. He answered these questions for me, but I know that I cannot tell you all that He said. A part of what He said is some of the lessons in the story that we have already covered, and other truths you may have gained as you have journeyed again with Abraham and his people.

But if you want to go deeper, let me just tell you that in regard to Ishmael, consider carefully what Scripture says in Romans 9. I had to cover my face and weep as God spoke His deep truth into my humbled heart:

> On the contrary, who are you, O man, who answers back to God? The thing molded will not say to the molder, "Why did you make me like this," will it? Or does not the potter have a right over the clay, to make from the same lump one vessel for honorable use, and another for common use? What if God, although willing to demonstrate His wrath and to make His power known, endured with much patience vessels of wrath prepared for destruction? And He did so to make known the riches of His glory upon vessels of mercy, which He prepared beforehand for glory, even us, whom He also called, not from among Jews only, but also from among Gentiles. Romans 9:20–24

My friend, I have studied Romans 9 in depth and could discuss it here, but I believe God wants an intimate moment with you, to teach you about His sovereignty and about who He is. The answers He gave me are in Romans chapters 9 through 11. May God bless you as you seek Him with all of your heart.

THE GOOD LIFE

I watched a story on TV about a group of people who went in together and bought lottery tickets. Well, they won the lottery, but the lady who actually went and got the tickets and was awarded the money would not share it with her friends. They had won over a million dollars.

Being friends, they sued her! If I am remembering correctly, the friends won the lawsuit and the lady had to share the money. But she appealed the court's decision and won the appeal, so the friends ended up with nothing.

They were interviewing the friends at the end of the show, and one lady said that she was single and had a son who was about twelve or thirteen years old, so having the money would have been great for them. I could tell that she was a Christian, because she was not resentful at all over the situation, and was thankful for her son, their health, and the life that they shared together.

When this mom told her son that they were not going to get the money, his response to her was priceless: "Mom, it would have been fun to have the money, but we have a good life just the way we are." She didn't cry, but I cried for her. That was so precious coming from her little boy.

They reminded me of Hagar and Ishmael. Rejected at such a tender time in life. They thought they had an inheritance, and then found out they had nothing. But they cried out to God and God heard them and showed them His compassion. They may not have gained the inheritance, but they had a pretty good life. Blessed be the name of the Lord.

LEARN THE LESSON

Here are a few of the lessons we learn from these people. The key questions to ask are: "What does God say?"

"What does God mean?" "How do I apply what He says and means to my life?" It does matter how we live, and by living by God's Word we can avoid most of the mud holes of life. Without this, we create little Ishmaels and end up hurting a lot of innocent people.

God's purposes and plans stand. He has created each of us for a reason. He created us with a free will, and He is doing all He can to draw us to Him. Yet, the free choice is ours. Because He is God, He knows already what choices we will make. He allows in our lives things that we may never understand.

God has promised to work all things together for good to those who love God, to those who are called according to His purpose (Rom. 8:28). If our desire is to know the good life, then we must simply let Him, in His own time and in His own way, bring about His will in our lives and in the lives of the people we love.

Chapter Eight

Preparing for Sacrifice

*T*erah, Lot, Sarah, Hagar, Ishmael: these persons played key supporting roles in the life of Abraham. We have seen how God used them in Abraham's life to teach him about Himself.

You are asking, I know, *What about Isaac? You forgot to talk about Isaac in the "people" chapter.* No, I didn't. You know a lot about Isaac already because of what God said about him before he was ever born.

Isaac was the heir to the promise, born to Abraham and Sarah when Abraham was 100 years old and Sarah was 90. Hey, they were young! Though Isaac was Sarah's only child, after Sarah died Abraham married Keturah, and she bore him six more children! He also had concubines that bore other sons for him (Gen. 25:1, 2, 6).

Nevertheless, he gave everything he had to Isaac and sent his other concubines and heirs off with nice "consolation prizes." Check this out: he sent them to live in the east, no doubt where Hagar and Ishmael had gone (Gen. 25:6). I hope he sent some gifts to Hagar and Ishmael. Water and bread—what was he thinking? You're right! He wasn't thinking.

We learn in chapter 22 that Isaac was the only person who made it to the place of sacrifice with Abraham, which I think is quite significant. Not even Sarah was there, and Abraham left his associates behind as he and Isaac traveled to the place of sacrifice.

Notice too that Scripture tells that Abraham left his donkey with his traveling companions. A donkey was an elite possession. Abraham was a very wealthy man and would have gladly given or sacrificed all he had in place of his son Isaac. But God did not ask for his stuff. Riches were not the dearest thing to Abraham's heart. His wife Sarah was not even the dearest thing to his heart. Isaac was, because he represented the Word of God, the promise of God, the blessing of God.

Isaac was a gift from God, but he was not God. What a lesson! While we love and appreciate and enjoy the gifts that God brings into our lives, these gifts are never greater than the Giver of every good and perfect gift. We must have a heart for God Himself—not just for His gifts. We must be willing to give God what He asks for and not just what we think He should have.

"God, I will give you this because it is very nice and very generous of me. This will help the cause of Christ in a greater way than anything else. Surely You are not asking me to do or to give that! You have given that to me, why would you want me to give it back?"

This is the rationale we use at certain times. But when we get to this point, God is probably asking for the very thing that we are reluctant to give up. The cause of Christ does not need our help. Jesus' finished work on Calvary and His resurrection three days later gives Him all He needs to be our Master. God is able to bring forth His will all by Himself. He is all-sufficient and self-sufficient. Remember? He is not working to improve Himself or His work in the earth. No, He is working in your heart and mine, making us more like His Son Jesus and drawing us to Himself. He is showing us where we are in our relationship with Him and is calling and drawing us into deeper intimacy.

He will test us in this. This testing is not designed for our failure, but for our advancement and for our good.

Remember one of the definitions of sacrifice: a sacrifice is the giving of a life or that which sustains life. A burnt offering is consumed totally. It is also given voluntarily, as a love offering. God was asking Abraham to give Him all of the best part of his life. It is the giving of our best.

This is what Isaac was to Abraham: the best part of his life. God knew that and used it in this final test of faith and obedience in the life of Father Abraham.

PREPARING FOR SACRIFICE

So, "after these things,"—after Abraham had gotten years into his process of faith and obedience and had grown greatly in his relationship with God, and after there was some resolution to the Ishmael-versus-Isaac controversy—Abraham was now being called to the ultimate test of faith.

> Now it came about after these things, that God tested Abraham, and said to him, "Abraham!" And he said, "Here I am."
>
> He said, "Take now your son, your only son, whom you love, Isaac, and go to the land of Moriah, and offer him there as a burnt offering on one of the mountains of which I will tell you."
>
> So Abraham rose early in the morning and saddled his donkey, and took two of his young men with him and Isaac his son; and he split wood for the burnt offering, and arose and went to the place of which God had told him.
> Genesis 22:1–3

Now get this: that very next morning Abraham loaded up what and whom he needed and headed toward the land of Moriah, to "one of the mountains of which I will tell you." Abraham had learned that God says what He means and means what He says. He heard God and responded immediately. I really like that!

"Early in the morning" always gets my attention

because I, and many of us women, understand the sacrifice that must be made by rising early in the morning. It's the time when the world is not doing its thing and our minds are not crowded. It's the time when we hear God most clearly. Everything around us is still, and we are focused.

I never want to lay a guilt trip on someone who does not rise early to meet with God on a consistent basis, because I know that we can meet with God at any time at all. However, I am in this thing called life right along with you, and I think that the best time to be about preparing ourselves for the Father's business is "early in the morning." How better can we live in response to God's Word than to begin each day with it?

Early in the morning, Abraham saddled his donkey. I remember one day rising early in the morning after being away for two weeks, saddling my donkey, and going to the place of sacrifice to which God had called me. I had been asked to sing for a group of first- through eighth-graders. I was very pregnant, not feeling well at all, and was very tired. But I knew that God had called me to share with these kids. The most precious thing to me that day was rest for my weary body, but God said, "Go." So I saddled my donkey—loading my car with everything I would need to have a great time with the students.

Abraham took two of his young men and Isaac. I took my nanny and my son Michael Chandler. I needed my nanny to help with my son, and I took him with me because God told me to.

Abraham told his young men to stay behind as he went up the mountain. I have learned a big lesson here. Others can help only so much. There is only so much advice and assistance we can get when we are called to the place of sacrifice. Once we see the place—that is, once we know exactly what God wants us to do—we have to leave behind those who are not directly involved in our act of obedience.

Abraham prepared himself for worship. He split the wood for the burnt offering. He could have asked his young men to do this for him, but splitting the wood was to be part of his worship experience.

I understand this on a small scale. When I arrived at the school, I had to clear the stage. Then I had to help with the sound check and the PowerPoint presentation.

I built the altar, and then God said, "Now get on it." He guided me as I shared biblical truth with this very diverse audience. As I allowed myself to be consumed by the fire of His presence, I saw that sweet little audience enter into worship, and my Father God was glorified.

At the end of the presentation, many prayed to receive Christ, and I do believe that their faith and prayers were sincere.

I could have done the program my way, and it might have been received very well. But I know that we would not have had the experience of intimacy with God that we did had I not been willing to rise early in the morning, saddle my donkey, take my young men and Isaac, split the wood, get on that altar, and allow God to consume my agenda so that we might enter into His.

This sacrificial offering led to eternal life for those who prayed to receive Christ. One teacher came to me after the meeting with tears in her eyes and told me how God had used that little chapel service to restore life and purpose in her. Her encouragement encouraged me. At that point, I really did understand that that morning was not about me at all. It was about God building His kingdom and graciously choosing me to be a part of His work. I shudder to think what I would have missed had I held on to me and my agenda. I am crucified with Christ, yet I live . . .

Oh yes, we can live sacrificially if we really want to. When we rise up early in the morning to listen for God's voice and prepare ourselves spiritually to follow in sacrificial obedience, we will hear the call to worship, the call to bow down and give life or that which sustains life every day.

PREPARING ISAAC

Isaac played the lead supporting role in this event, yet he never got a script. The script was given to Abraham alone. At least, that is all that we know from God's Word. If God had wanted us to know differently, He would have given us more or different information. This script was given to Abraham, and he had to engage others without even telling them what their roles were or what the plot would be.

That was probably a good thing, because Abraham did not know how this drama would play out. We know that he was a man of faith, that he believed God, that God called him righteous. We know from Hebrews 11 that Abraham is honored for his deep faith.

But what about Isaac? He was called to the place of worship, but he had not heard from God. He was only being obedient to his father and following his instructions.

I believe we can learn a lot of great things about Isaac from Genesis 22. Throughout the passage, Isaac never argued with his father. He was obedient to rise early and help his father prepare for the journey.

The journey is a long and quiet one. They traveled for three days, and on the third day, when Abraham saw the place, he told his men to stay while he and Isaac would "go yonder" to worship and then would return. Abraham had known for three days that he was to offer Isaac, his only son, as a sacrifice. However, on this third day he clearly stated that they would worship and return. What a man! What a heart! What a faith!

Isaac heard this, and as he and his dad continued the journey to worship and return, Isaac asked one question, to which Abraham gave him a simple answer. "Isaac spoke to Abraham his father and said, 'My father!' And he said, 'Here I am, my son.' And he said, 'Behold, the fire and the wood, but where is the lamb for the burnt offering?' Abraham said, 'God will provide for Himself the lamb for the burnt offering, my son.' So the two of them walked on together" (Gen. 22:7–8).

From this statement, you know that Isaac knew what it meant to worship. One must have a lamb for a burnt offering. He knew this because his father has taught him how to worship God correctly.

We can have fire and we can have wood, but rest assured, without the Lamb we will never worship God in Spirit and in Truth.

Abraham's response is brilliant! After three days of thinking about this and making his way to the land of Moriah, which means "Jehovah provides," Abraham answered, "God will provide for Himself," which can be translated, God will provide Himself, the Lamb. Awesome! The Word of God is awesome! Hallelujah! The Word of God is a living and breathing reality. Oh, taste and see that the Lord is good!

Isaac took Abraham's answer into his heart, and they proceeded up the mountain to the place of sacrifice.

When they came to the place of which God had told him, Abraham built an altar. Isaac could have done it, but Abraham did it. Isaac was just watching his dad obey God. Abraham arranged the wood. Then Abraham bound his son! Abraham laid him on the altar on top of the wood. Abraham stretched out his hand and took the knife to slay his son. Isaac said nothing.

Isaac was big, strong, and mature enough to resist, but he did not. He did not say a word. He trusted his father. "God will provide. We will worship and return."

In this story we see a picture of Jesus, when He was to be offered as a living sacrifice for us.

> Let us run with endurance the race that is set before us, fixing our eyes on Jesus, the author and perfecter of faith, who for the joy set before Him endured the cross, despising the shame, and has sat down at the right hand of the throne of God. Hebrews 12:1–2

For the joy set before us, we can endure the cross, despise the shame, bind and lay our Isaacs on the altar we have built at God's bidding. We can play our role in the act of sacrifice and worship because we know we will worship and return, and God will provide.

Sacrifice is not about our will or our agenda. It is about doing God's will. We can go the distance. We can live in sacrificial obedience if we will but fix our eyes on Jesus. He is the author and perfecter of our faith.

Therefore, preparation begins with the Word of God: praying the Word, memorizing the Word, and meditating on the Word. Then we are to obey fully and immediately. We must hide God's Word in our hearts so that we might not sin against Him. Preparation takes time and is the first part of sacrifice.

Prepare daily, and at any given point in time, you will be ready to make the sacrifice God calls you to. Remember that we are to be living sacrifices, holy, pleasing, and acceptable to God. This is our reasonable act of service and worship.

Blessed be the name of the Lord!

Chapter Nine

Place of Sacrifice

*W*hy was God so specific about the land of Moriah? Why so far away? Why on a mountain top? What was so significant about the land of Moriah?

Moriah is quite significant, as we will see in a moment. But remember, God is not indifferent about anything. He has a specific plan and purpose for everything, and He is passionate about it. I am thankful that He does not hide His commands and leave us guessing. When He wants us to get up and go, He is very specific about what we are to do at the given moment, even if He says, "Go to the land and I will show you the place." That should be enough to move us from where we are to where He wants us to be. Are you ready to go to the land of Moriah? Here we go.

As we have learned, the name *Moriah* means "Jehovah provides." That's a huge blessing to my heart. We can know from the start that when we are called to the land of Moriah, the place of sacrifice, it is the place where Jehovah provides. If Abraham understood Moriah in this way when God spoke to him, then I can understand why he immediately obeyed the Lord.

Not only was the place in the land of Moriah, but it was on a mountain that God would show him. Abraham had to keep looking up toward heaven as he sought the place that God was calling him to. You and I must do the same. Our eyes and our hearts must stay set on our God until He shows us the place He is calling us to.

It is so easy to go to the place that the insurance company provides, or the HMO provides, or the job provides, or the relationships provide. But the place of sacrifice is a place where Jehovah provides. Already, this is where I want to be.

The place was also three days away from Abraham's current location. Three days away would have been out and away from the interests and affairs of his family, friends, and life as he knew it.

The place was not influenced by his business associates and friends because Abraham, after getting the help he needed, asked them to wait in a particular place while he and his son Isaac went "yonder." Yonder was a place further and deeper, beyond where Abraham's associates and friends were able to go; further and deeper and higher, where God had prepared only the hearts of Abraham and Isaac to go.

It was a place of worship, sacrifice, and deep intimacy with God. It is the place where a holy God meets with mortal man and the course of man's life is changed forever.

It's a place in the heart—high above and far away from the interests and cares of the world. It's the place where we, in sacrificial obedience, bow the knee and the heart and say, "Yes, Lord."

A PLACE OUTSIDE

It is also the place where a Father would one day provide Himself, the Lamb, the Lord Jesus Christ, for the sins of all humankind. It is a holy place. The land of Moriah!

> For the bodies of those animals whose blood is brought into the holy place by the high priest as an offering for sin, are burned outside the camp. Therefore Jesus also, that He might sanctify the people through His own blood, suffered outside the gate. So, let us go out to Him outside the camp, bearing His reproach. Hebrews 13:11–13

The key phrase repeated in these verses is "outside the camp." It seems God wants us to know something about being outside the camp. Here we learn that the blood was brought into the holy place by the high priest. These animal carcasses were then burned outside the camp, far and away from the holy temple.

Now Jesus, who is our High Priest, has brought His precious blood into the Heavenly tabernacle, having been sacrificed on Calvary, once for all, outside the city gate, outside the interest of world systems, and far away from religion, that he might sanctify us and make us holy.

Hence, we who are in Christ Jesus and called according to His purpose are called to the place of sacrifice outside the camp—out and away from the ways of the world and its agendas, apart from the routine way of doing things—that we might be brought near to the presence of God, into intimacy with Him.

Not only is the place of sacrifice far away from the interests of the world, but it is also the place where we die to self and God brings new life. I know you are beginning to see this by now. The place of sacrifice is the place where we hold nothing back, but rather we die daily so that our sacrificial obedience might bring us to a deeper, more intimate place of worship of our Lord.

A PLACE OF PROVISION

If you do not know the story of Abraham's sacrifice of his son Isaac, you can read it in Genesis 22.

The drama of this sacrifice ends when Abraham stretches out his hand to slay his son, and God calls out to him again.

> But the angel of the Lord called to him from heaven and said, "Abraham, Abraham!" And he said, "Here I am."

He said, "Do not stretch out your hand against the lad, and do nothing to him; for now I know that you fear God, since you have not withheld your son, your only son, from Me." Genesis 22:11–12

Here is an interesting note for you. Killing a first-born son was not an uncommon practice in the days of Abraham. There was much idolatry during that day, and killing a first-born son in honor of an idol was considered a very noble practice. If nothing else, God was asking Abraham, *Do you love Me more than these who are following false gods? Will you honor and love Me with complete obedience?*

Abraham had the faith to become the father of Isaac but now came the ultimate challenge of his faith. Would he love God more than he loved Isaac and become the father of the family of all those who would come to faith in the Lord Jesus Christ? The answer is *Yes*. Abraham was in the place where God provides, and he believed that God kept His promises. The death of Isaac would mean God's promise was not true. God's Word has never failed and never will fail. Abraham believed all of what God had promised to him.

The angel of the Lord said, "I know that you fear God, since you have not withheld your son, your only son, from Me." God was not after Isaac's heart; He was after Abraham's heart.

God's plan and purpose for this sacrifice was complete. Abraham showed forth a greater love for God, becoming not only the father of Isaac, but the father of the faithful. Isaac is a picture of what you and I are called to be: a living sacrifice (Rom. 12:1–2).

Then Abraham raised his eyes and looked, and behold, behind him a ram caught in the thicket by his horns; and Abraham went and took the ram and offered him up for a burnt offering in the place of his son.

> Abraham called the name of that place The LORD Will Provide, as it is said to this day, "In the mount of the LORD it will be provided." Genesis 22:13–14

This is where we get the name *Jehovah Jireh*, God our Provider. *Jireh* is actually translated "to see." How then do we get "provide"? God sees, therefore He foresees, therefore He provides. Think about that for a moment.

In the land of Moriah, the place of sacrifice, God sees, foresees, and provides.

He provided for Abraham and He will provide for you. Don't be afraid to give Him your Isaac. Hold nothing back. Sacrificial obedience leads to intimacy with God and moves on toward the greater plan that God has for our lives. Keep your eyes on the place, and you will see the Person, Jehovah Jireh, our great Provider.

A PLACE OF LOVE

The land of Moriah is a place of obedience, sacrifice, and worship. It is a place outside the interests of the world, a place where God provides. It is a holy place; it is also a place of love.

The land of Moriah, the place where Abraham was to sacrifice Isaac, has been traditionally identified as the place where the temple mount is located in Jerusalem today (2 Chron. 3:1). The temple mount, or the Dome of the Rock, today is the site of a Muslim mosque built in A.D. 691. Inside the mosque there is a portion of the rock where it is believed that Abraham had intended to sacrifice Isaac.

Yet just beyond the walls of the temple mount, on the same mountain range, on a hill called Golgotha, or in Latin, *Calvary*, God did not spare His son, but delivered Him up for us all (Rom. 8:32).

Abraham demonstrated his love for God by raising his hand to slay his son in obedience to Him. God demonstrates His love for us in that while we were yet sinners, Christ died for us (Rom. 5:8).

For God so loved the world that He held nothing back, but gave—sacrificially gave—His only begotten Son whom He loved, that whoever would believe that Jesus is the Son of God would not perish, but would be granted God's free gift, His Holy Spirit, Eternal Life (John 3:16).

The land of Moriah: a place of love! Hold nothing back. Demonstrate your love for God. Make the sacrifices He asks of you. Give Him your Isaac. Let love be the fuel that fires your engine of obedient faith.

Abraham was justified by works and not by meaningless faith alone. As a result of his works, his faith was made perfect (James 2:22). This is what we want, and it comes through complete obedience, motivated by love for God.

God knows the heart. May He say to you what He said to Abraham: "Now I know that you fear God."

A PLACE OF PEACE

The land of Moriah, I have found, is also a place of peace.

Can we talk for just a minute?

As I am writing this, I am seven months pregnant. My first pregnancy was fabulous. Uneventful, easy labor and delivery—it was wonderful. This pregnancy has been the same, until today. Today, I was about to board an airplane heading toward Jacksonville, Florida, when I realized that something was not normal with my body.

I was on my cell phone, talking with a girlfriend who was telling me that she, too, was pregnant. As I was rejoicing with her, I heard my flight being called. I deliberated whether to get onto the flight or to stop and pay attention to my body, which was not functioning as it should have been.

I chose to check out the situation before boarding the plane, and found out that I had started to bleed abnormally. I was scared out of my mind.

Right then and there, I knew that I was called to the place of sacrifice. Would I board the plane and hope the bleeding stopped? Should I go on to the conference and just go to a doctor there? The ladies were expecting me to speak and sing; what was I to do? We needed the money—I'm going to be off work for a while when the baby comes, so I need to work as much as I can now. I needed to go and just let a doctor see me when I got there. The ladies needed me and I needed them.

Then I realized that the place of sacrifice is the place where God provides. He would provide for the conference, and He would provide for me. I was still a little panicked, but I let the ticket agent know that I was having a medical emergency and would not be boarding the plane. I asked her to get my bags off, and I immediately went to my car.

I drove around to the luggage area for the bags. They were not there. So I left and drove off to get my husband.

Before I reached Richard, I could not hold back the tears; I did not want to lose my baby or deliver him too soon. Immediately I remembered the sovereignty of God and that He controls all things. He knows when we will come into the world, and He knows when and how we will leave.

I knew the baby would probably be okay, but I just could not bear the thought of him having to fight so hard for his life right from the start.

I did not want Richard to see me falling apart, so I placed the situation in God's hands. I told Him that whatever the outcome would be, I would always love Him and trust His sovereignty.

I let His good, good Word dwell deeply and richly in my heart. I dried my eyes, picked up Richard, and off we went to see the doctor.

During the examination and ultrasound, nothing abnormal was found. The baby was fine and I was fine. The bleeding we still cannot explain.

I was told to rest for several days, and if there were no more abnormalities, I could resume a "normal" life. Normal for me is abnormal, so that really meant that I needed to slow down just a little.

I had to cancel my appearance at the meeting, which ripped my heart out. I love to sing. I love to speak. I love this ministry. I have even struggled with being a wife and mother because of the sacrifices I have to make, because these responsibilities come before ministry. Now, being pregnant with a second baby, these thoughts and feelings have resurfaced.

I work in a very competitive industry, and if you don't show up, somebody else will. Out of sight is out of mind, according to world systems. To cancel my speaking engagement seemed out of the question. But there was no question about it: I was called to the place of sacrifice, a place outside the gate, and canceling was my only alternative.

Once the issue was resolved, I lifted my eyes and saw the place, the land of Moriah, where God provides!

I stretched out my hand for the cell phone, dialed the number, and canceled my appearance. The voice on the other end had many kind and understanding things to say. But all I heard was the still, sweet voice of my Lord saying, "Peace."

In the land of Moriah, you will find peace. You may not know the reason for the disappointment or abnormality, but you can know His peace.

Peace is a person, and His name is Jesus Christ, the Prince of Peace. He is the sovereign God who controls all things. Nothing takes Him by surprise. Nothing happens in our lives before passing through His sovereign hands.

When called to the place of sacrifice, remember that it is in the land of Moriah, the place where God provides, outside of the cares and expectations of world systems. It is a very holy place, a place of love, and a place of peace.

A PLACE OF PROMISE

Here in the land of Moriah, after seeing and receiving Abraham's love, obedience, and worship, God not only restated His promise to Abraham, but declared an oath to go with it. Because there was no name greater that he could swear by, God swore by His own name that He would bless Abraham greatly for the love that he had shown toward His name: "By Myself I have sworn, declares the LORD, because you have done this thing and have not withheld your son, your only son, indeed I will greatly bless you, and I will greatly multiply your seed as the stars of the heavens and as the sand which is on the seashore; and your seed shall possess the gate of their enemies. In your seed all the nations of the earth shall be blessed, because you have obeyed My voice" (Gen. 22:16–18).

God had already told Abraham that He would bless him if he obeyed. After years of instructing and teaching Abraham in the way that he should go and seeing his faith put into action, God said, "I will greatly bless you and greatly multiply you."

What a great God we serve. God is faithful to His promise. Not only is Abraham the father of Isaac, but he is the father of all those, from any and every nation, who come to a saving faith in the Lord Jesus Christ (Rom. 4).

GOD: OUR JUST REWARDER

I cannot help but think of the day I got a little upset with God because He gave Esther and Mordecai everything, and it seemed like I loved Him more and did more for Him, but I was not being rewarded for my faith and work. Someone else always got picked. I never got picked. I have told you that story in chapter four.

Here is what I now know. I have seen this in the story of Abraham, and I have seen this in my own life, over and over again: "God is not unjust so as to forget your work and the love which you have shown toward His name, in having ministered and in still ministering to the saints" (Heb. 6:10). And "every good thing given and every perfect gift is from above, coming down from the Father of lights, with whom there is no variation or shifting shadow" (James 1:17). "Without faith it is impossible to please Him, for he who comes to God must believe that He is and that He is a rewarder of those who seek Him" (Heb. 11:6).

Look at these verses again, and make a little list of what they say about God. Use this list as you offer up the sacrifice of praise, the fruit of your lips, giving thanks to His name. Blessed be the name of the Lord!

Chapter Ten

Princesses of Sacrifice

*O*ur discussion of Abraham and his story have been wonderful. There we see perfect examples of sacrifice and developing true intimacy with God. We have also noted some key New Testament Scriptures pointing us to the truth of the Old Testament and the fulfillment of the ultimate sacrifice in Jesus Christ. Hopefully by now we understand the foolishness of holding anything back from Him! Intimacy with the God of all creation is ours if we will obey!

In this chapter, I'd like us to look at two women who aren't from the story of Abraham but have incredible testimonies of sacrifice and true closeness to God. My inclusion of these characters may surprise you, but I like to call them Princesses of Sacrifice. I love these women and their stories. Learn from them along with me.

> In the same way, was not Rahab the harlot also justified by works when she received the messengers and sent them out by another way? James 2:25

Rahab? Rahab the harlot? Now wait a minute, Alicia. What do you suppose a bad girl like Rahab can teach us good girls about sacrificial obedience leading to intimacy with God?

Well, sweet darling, you just hang on to your "goodgirlness" and let me take you for a stroll down God's great hall of "goodgirlness and grace."

RAHAB THE HARLOT

First of all, take note that there are only two women listed in Hebrews 11, God's Hall of Faith: Sarah (verse 11) and—you guessed it—Rahab the harlot. "By faith Rahab the harlot did not perish along with those who were disobedient, after she had welcomed the spies in peace" (verse 31).

Rahab believed in the God of Israel, held nothing back, and was sacrificially obedient to God's servants, thereby finding peace and intimacy with God. Her story is told in Joshua 2. Let's read it together. It really is a great story.

> Then Joshua the son of Nun sent two men as spies secretly from Shittim, saying, "Go, view the land, especially Jericho." So they went and came into the house of a harlot whose name was Rahab, and lodged there.
>
> It was told the king of Jericho, saying, "Behold, men from the sons of Israel have come here tonight to search out the land."
>
> And the king of Jericho sent word to Rahab, saying, "Bring out the men who have come to you, who have entered your house, for they have come to search out all the land."
>
> But the woman had taken the two men and hidden them, and she said, "Yes, the men came to me, but I did not know where they were from.
>
> "It came about when it was time to shut the gate at dark, that the men went out; I do not know where the men went. Pursue them quickly, for you will overtake them."
>
> But she had brought them up to the roof and hidden them in the stalks of flax which she had laid in order on the roof.
>
> So the men pursued them on the road to the Jordan to the fords; and as soon as those who were pursuing them had gone out, they shut the gate.

Now before they lay down, she came up to them on the roof, and said to the men, "I know that the LORD has given you the land, and that the terror of you has fallen on us, and that all the inhabitants of the land have melted away before you.

"For we have heard how the Lord dried up the water of the Red Sea before you when you came out of Egypt, and what you did to the two kings of the Amorites who were beyond the Jordan, to Sihon and Og, whom you utterly destroyed.

"When we heard it, our hearts melted and no courage remained in any man any longer because of you; for the LORD your God, He is God in heaven above and on earth beneath.

"Now therefore, please swear to me by the LORD, since I have dealt kindly with you, that you also will deal kindly with my father's household, and give me a pledge of truth, and spare my father and my mother and my brothers and my sisters, with all who belong to them, and deliver our lives from death."

So the men said to her, "Our life for yours if you do not tell this business of ours; and it shall come about when the LORD gives us the land that we will deal kindly and faithfully with you."

Then she let them down by a rope through the window, for her house was on the city wall, so that she was living on the wall.

She said to them, "Go to the hill country, so that the pursuers will not happen upon you, and hide yourselves there for three days until the pursuers return. Then afterward you may go on your way."

The men said to her, "We shall be free from this oath to you which you have made us swear, unless, when we come into the land, you tie this cord of scarlet thread in the window through which you let us down, and gather to yourself into the house your father and your mother and your brothers and all your father's household.

"It shall come about that anyone who goes out of the doors of your house into the street, his blood shall be on his own head, and we shall be free; but anyone who is with you in the house, his blood shall be on our head if a hand is laid on him.

"But if you tell this business of ours, then we shall be free from the oath which you have made us swear."

She said, "According to your words, so be it." So she sent them away, and they departed; and she tied the scarlet cord in the window.

They departed and came to the hill country, and remained there for three days until the pursuers returned. Now the pursuers had sought them all along the road, but had not found them.

Then the two men returned and came down from the hill country and crossed over and came to Joshua the son of Nun, and they related to him all that had happened to them.

They said to Joshua, "Surely the Lord has given all the land into our hands; moreover, all the inhabitants of the land have melted away before us." Joshua 2:1–24

Hebrews tells us that Rahab had faith and that she was obedient. Joshua 2:9–11 shows us what Rahab believed. Take a moment and review those verses.

Rahab's knowledge of God produced faith, and her sacrificial obedient response was to hide the spies so that they would not be killed by the men of Jericho.

She risked it all—her home, her family, her life—but she feared God more than she feared anyone or anything else. She knew that God is the Great Deliverer, and that He had delivered and fought for Israel and was no doubt going to do the same for them again. This meant that she and her family were doomed unless they could somehow ally themselves with Israel.

Instead of setting herself against the spies and the work of God, Rahab chose sacrificial obedience. She then asked to be spared from destruction, and that is exactly what she got—not only for herself but for her family who came in to her house.

> Joshua said to the two men who had spied out the land, "Go into the harlot's house and bring the woman and all she has out of there, as you have sworn to her."
> So the young men who were spies went in and brought out Rahab and her father and her mother and her brothers and all she had; they also brought out all her relatives and placed them outside the camp of Israel.
> They burned the city with fire, and all that was in it. Only the silver and gold, and articles of bronze and iron, they put into the treasury of the house of the LORD.
> However, Rahab the harlot and her father's household and all she had, Joshua spared; and she has lived in the midst of Israel to this day, for she hid the messengers whom Joshua sent to spy out Jericho. Joshua 6:22–25

Rahab made the Hall of Faith! She is not remembered for her harlotry, but for her faith and obedience. And guess what! Her legacy does not end there. Rahab is an ancestor of the Lord Jesus Christ. Go figure! There she is again in Matthew 1:5. She is the mother of Boaz, who is the great grandfather of King David. She is David's great, great grandmother. David is the father of Solomon and ancestor to Joseph, the husband of Mary and Jesus' earthly father.

Rahab, a Canaanite harlot, now a Princess of Sacrifice, shows us how to achieve intimacy with God. She simply heard the Word of God and chose to faithfully respond to it. Rahab chose sacrificial obedience and received a place in the kingdom of God and in the lineage of Jesus Christ. The place of obedient sacrifice is a place of deliverance, safety, blessing, and eternal intimacy with God.

THE SINFUL WOMAN

There is one other woman I want to leave you with. She is one of my favorite persons in all of Scripture. She has no name, so I like to use my name, and you can use your name if you like.

Her story is told only once in God's Word, in Luke 7. Every other listing of a similar account is about Mary of Bethany, the sister of Martha and Lazarus. But this lady is mentioned only once, and she is nameless.

Different translations of the Bible describe her with different words. She is called an especially "wicked sinner" in the Amplified Bible. Verse 39 describes her as "a notorious sinner," "a social outcast, devoted to sin." If you want a more dignified way of describing her, the New Living Translation will help you. There she is referred to as "a certain immoral woman."

I like the New American Standard Bible, which refers to her simply as a "sinner." Sin is sin, and we get into trouble when we start to classify it. All sin separates us from the love of God. Jesus died to take away all the sin of the world. It does not matter what her sins were or what your or my sins are. All have sinned and come short of intimacy with God. Sinful! That is what she was. That is what you and I are. This could be your story. This could be mine.

There was a dinner at the home of Simon the Pharisee, and this woman heard that Jesus was there.

> Now one of the Pharisees was requesting Him [Jesus] to dine with him, and He entered the Pharisee's house and reclined at the table.
> And there was a woman in the city who was a sinner; and when she learned that He was reclining at the table in the Pharisee's house, she brought an alabaster vial of perfume, and standing behind Him at His feet, weeping, she

began to wet His feet with her tears, and kept wiping them with the hair of her head, and kissing His feet and anointing them with the perfume. Luke 7:36–38

This seemed totally out of order. Look at the response of Simon, the host:

Now when the Pharisee who had invited Him saw this, he said to himself, "If this man were a prophet He would know who and what sort of person this woman is who is touching Him, that she is a sinner."

And Jesus answered him, "Simon, I have something to say to you." And he replied, "Say it, Teacher."

"A moneylender had two debtors: one owed five hundred denarii, and the other fifty. When they were unable to repay, he graciously forgave them both. So which of them therefore will love him more?"

Simon answered and said, "I suppose the one whom he forgave more." And He said to him, "You have judged correctly."

Turning toward the woman, He said to Simon, "Do you see this woman? I entered your house; you gave Me no water for My feet, but she has wet My feet with her tears and wiped them with her hair.

"You gave Me no kiss; but she, since the time I came in, has not ceased to kiss My feet.

"You did not anoint My head with oil, but she anointed My feet with perfume.

"For this reason I say to you, her sins, which are many, have been forgiven, for she loved much; but he who is forgiven little, loves little."

Then He said to her, "Your sins have been forgiven."

Those who were reclining at the table with Him began to say to themselves, "Who is this man who even forgives sins?"

And He said to the woman, "Your faith has saved you; go in peace." Luke 7:39–50

This woman's actions totally interrupted the gathering. Simon's first response was to question who Jesus really was (verse 39). Jesus knew what Simon was thinking (Jesus knows all things), and—get this—Jesus answered him, even though Simon had not said a word. Jesus answered his thoughts. I love that!

Then Jesus gave a parable that is very easy to answer. (Thank you, Jesus, because some of Your parables are a little difficult to grasp.) This one is not difficult. I got the answer right, and so did Simon. One who has been forgiven much is going to love much. One who has been forgiven little is going to love little.

Simon saw the woman's actions as an interruption. Jesus saw the situation completely differently. There is a lesson in this for us. When we plan a meeting or a worship experience and invite Jesus to be there, we must be careful how we respond to those who respond to Him with acts of love that are different from ours. Jesus saw this woman's heart as well as her actions.

After Simon answered correctly, Jesus turned toward the woman, who was still at His feet, wetting them with her tears and drying them with her hair and anointing them with her perfume. He then gave His analysis of the situation.

Jesus explained to Simon that he had greeted Him improperly. Let alone the fact that he was entertaining God, Simon had slipped in his duties as a host. He had failed to offer water for Jesus' feet, which any gracious host would do in that day. Yet this woman had wet Jesus' feet with her tears.

You may ask, why tears? Why was she crying so? If you can grasp how precious her tears are, then you will have begun to understand the holiness of God. These tears recognized Jesus' perfect holiness and her utter sinfulness. His holy and sinless presence exposes our unholiness and sin-fulness. This brings true repentance in the one longing for the new life that He offers, and such repentance is accom-panied by an overflow of grateful tears. She was overcome with Jesus' grace and love.

Simon had offered no towel, but this "sinful woman" had dried Jesus' feet with her hair. Oh yes, she let her hair down, big time! She came to Him in a totally unconven-tional way, not caring about the order of service or what was considered proper protocol by the people attending. She was not really invited or even welcomed. But the less fortunate were allowed at such gatherings, in order that they might catch a few crumbs or scraps from the table. She let her hair down, dried His feet, and then poured her precious perfume on them.

She broke the mold of tradition, symbolized by a com-mon alabaster vial, and poured out her most precious offering on the feet of Jesus. She poured, meaning she recklessly abandoned herself to Him. She poured out her life at His feet. That perfume may have been that which she wore on her body as a means of drawing attention to herself and luring men into her way of life. This was her survival, this was her life, and she poured it all out at the Savior's feet. What a sacrifice!

In the accounts of Mary of Bethany during a similar act of worship, all the attention is given to the price of the oil: 300 denarii—a year's salary. There is no mention of the price of this woman's oil, for it is priceless. This was her life.

Simon offered no oil for Jesus' head, which again, any gracious host would have done. Nor did he greet Jesus with a kiss. These were a part of protocol, the responsibili-ties of any host, and Simon had failed to do any of these things.

Yet this sinful woman did not cease to kiss Jesus' feet. I want you to see her heart of worship. She was sinful, and probably knew very little, if anything, about worship or church protocol. Yet she knew what was in her heart, and she followed her heart. Worship is not taught—it is caught! Can I say it again? *Worship is caught, not taught!* She kissed His feet. She was caught up in the moment and totally consumed by His awesome presence. This is a picture of biblical worship.

Worship involves bowing down to God. Lived out in the events of life, it is to live with a bowed-down heart before God. The most common word for worship in the New Testament is *proskuneo*, which means "to kiss," to fawn or crouch, to prostrate oneself in homage, to pay reverence, to adore.

This is exactly what this sinful woman did. She had obviously heard about Jesus, and what she had heard produced the faith she needed to make her way to where He was. Once in the place, His holy presence brought forth a repentant heart that melted away her former hardness of heart into tears of repentance, love, and worship.

Her tears were enough to wash His tired, dusty feet. She let go of who she was and dried His feet with her hair, kissing them over and over again in love and thanksgiving.

Finally, she sacrificially poured out upon His feet the best she had to offer. She brought to Him a priceless gift— her very best material possession. But more importantly she gave Him her life. Jesus forgave her sins and offered her His life, eternal life. "And He said to the woman, 'Your faith has saved you; go in peace'" (Luke 7:50).

Saved like Abraham, saved like Rahab, saved like the apostles, saved like Billy Graham, saved like you and me— from the guttermost to the uttermost! This woman was saved by her faith, displayed in this sacrificial act of worship. "Go live in peace," Jesus commanded her. Live at peace with yourself and with God. Your sins are forgiven, your faith has saved you, go in peace.

Peace is an inward sense of goodness unrelated to circumstances. It is undisturbed and untroubled well-being, but not an absence of outward turmoil. God's presence is my peace. Yes, I know the Peace Speaker by name.

Scripture offers no response from anyone after Luke 7:50. Great! There doesn't need to be one. Jesus had received her sacrificial worship, had forgiven her sins, and told her that her faith had saved her. His Word is forever settled.

The woman has no name here; she could be you, she could be me. The beauty of her story is that she followed her heart and caught true worship. She sacrificially gave her all to Jesus, and He in turn gave her all of Himself: "Your faith has *saved* you." She was no longer a "sinful woman," but was now a forgiven woman, our beautiful Princess _____. You fill in the name.

Did you put your name there? Great, if you did. If not, why not? All have sinned and fallen short of God's glory.

I pray that you will hear the Word of the Lord and go to the place in your heart where He is drawing you. I pray that you will, in total faith and obedience, pour your life out at His feet and let Him forgive your sins and give you His life eternal.

The woman in our story used no words, but her deeds and body posture showed the position of her heart. She was repentant and recklessly abandoned to Jesus. She was a sinner, and she recognized her need for the Savior. She was "justified by faith," and her faith was made perfect by her works.

Hear what Paul had to say to the church in Rome:

But what does it say? "THE WORD IS NEAR YOU, IN YOUR MOUTH AND IN YOUR HEART"—that is, the word of faith which we are preaching, that if you confess with your mouth Jesus as Lord, and believe in your heart that God raised Him from the dead, you will be saved; for with the heart a person believes, resulting in righteousness, and with the mouth he confesses, resulting in salvation. Romans 10:8–10

Words are great when they are accompanied by the good deeds of faith. Without faith your words are meaningless. Without faith it is impossible to please God. Your faith will produce a sacrificial act of obedience, and that perfected faith will save you.

For those of you who have already received life in Jesus' name, I encourage you to *hold nothing back*! Let sacrificial obedience bring you into an ongoing intimate relationship with God. You have been surrounded with a great cloud of witnesses. Now, immediately and with reckless abandon, lay aside every encumbrance and the sin that so easily entangles. Hold nothing back! Run with endurance the race that is set before you. Fix your eyes on Jesus, the author and perfecter of your faith (Heb. 12:1–2).

Grace and peace!

Conclusion

We have come to the ending of the book, but I hope you won't stop here in your journey to the altar of sacrificial obedience. There is much more that can be said, and I trust and pray that these thoughts have helped to open your hearts and minds to what it means to be a living sacrifice—holy, pleasing, and acceptable to God.

There is nothing—absolutely nothing—more rewarding. I have tried living according to my own rules or the rules of someone else, as I am sure you have. I am also sure that we have come to the same conclusion: life is in God alone, and sacrificial obedience leads to that life. God's thoughts and ways are higher than ours; they are also better for us than our own. Not only are they better, they are best.

God does not see life as we do. He does not stand on a street curb, as we would, and watch life go by, one event at a time like we watch floats in a parade. No! He is high and lifted up! He is a holy God. He sees the entire parade of life, at all times, from beginning to end. He knows what has happened, what is happening, and what is to come. Nothing takes Him by surprise.

He knows what is going on in our lives, so He is not watching the parade like we are. He is more interested in watching us. He is interested in our response to the events that come our way.

Though nothing surprises Him or catches Him off guard, He is moved in His heart when He sees us respond in faith to the circumstances in our lives.

If you read the Gospels, you will see that Jesus is always moved in His heart when one chooses to believe in God and respond to life in faith.

The just shall live by faith. Without faith it is impossible to please God. Those who come to God must believe that He exists as God and that He is the Rewarder of those who seek Him. "Every God-begotten person conquers the world's ways. The conquering power that brings the world to its knees is our *faith*. The person who wins out over the world's ways is simply the one who *believes* Jesus is the Son of God" (*The Message*).

We have talked about this in one of my favorite chapters, "Power of Faith in Sacrifice." We must respond in sacrificial, obedient faith to the events and circumstances of our lives. Faith comes from hearing and knowing God's Word (Rom. 10:17).

Abraham was justified by his works when he offered up Isaac his son on the altar. "You see that faith was working with his works, and as a result of the works, faith was perfected; and the Scripture was fulfilled which says, 'AND ABRAHAM BELIEVED GOD, AND IT WAS RECKONED TO HIM AS RIGHTEOUSNESS,' and he was called the friend of God. You see that a man is justified by works, and not by faith alone" (James 2:21–24).

God is interested in our response, in what we do with the faith we say we have. As Christians, as believers who are holding nothing back from God, we can change not only ourselves but our nation and world.

PATRIOTISM AND SACRIFICE

Has the United States been called to the place of sacrifice? Are the tragedies that we face as a nation, such as the events of September 11, 2001, a call to the land of Moriah? We say and sing "God Bless America," but our call really is for America to stand up and bless God.

I have deep questions about which I am very passionate. When will we call sin sin and stop justifying our sin with political correctness? When will the church in America stand up for Jesus? What will it take to get God's people to the polls to vote for an agenda that resembles the heart of God? Voting is a gift from God and should be used to honor His Word and His name.

When will church folks once again seek the face of God? When will the church stop expecting the government to do the work that we are called by God to do? Do we pray for our country and our leaders as God has commanded us to do?

Think about the moral fiber of our country today— the things we see on television, on the Internet, in magazines, and what we hear on the radio and see on billboards. We have total access to impurity, and the fight to stay pure gets tougher every day. Nevertheless, we must not give up the fight.

We must pray for America on a daily basis. And even though I believe that America is the best land on the face of the earth, she is not perfect. We have our downfalls and things we could do better, as a nation and as individuals. The responsibility to improve does not rest on the shoulders of one person or group; it is our responsibility to live in a way that will bless God.

Are we blessing God when we support things that He opposes? What are we teaching our children? We must teach them right from wrong and that there are absolutes, because God says so! Teach them Holy Scripture, because His Word is truth, His Word is forever settled in the heavens, Holy Scripture has never failed and never will fail, His Word stands, and His Word is the final judge.

We cannot teach the Word until we know the Word. That is why I am such an avid promoter of daily Bible study. We have to make God's Word central and first in our lives if we are going to see a nation of people who will truly stand up and bless God.

God's Word is His power and it has the power to bring about biblical and eternal change on a national and personal level. Through conflict that we have endured as a nation since September 11, 2001, I have seen a return to God and a biblical way of thinking and living. I have sensed a fear and awe of God that I do not remember having seen before in my lifetime. This is good. This is very good. But will it last?

Or will we be like Israel in the book of Judges: when we are hurting and struggling we call on God and promise to live right. When He blesses us, we forget Him and His ways, and fall back into sin.

Yes, God Bless America, but let me shout it from the mountain tops: America, let's stand up and bless God!

Prayers of the Righteous

As we pray not only for our nation, but for our world and others around us, we will see God's power reign supreme. We can affect the lives of others, of whole countries, as they too fall on their faces at the altars to which God is leading them. The fervent prayers of the righteous have an effect. The effect moves on beyond motivation and brings about a change of life. The change is biblical and eternal.

There is power in God's Words to us, and when we pray His Word, we can expect change. Praying the Word is praying in the name and nature of Jesus Christ. Jesus says when we pray in His name, we have what we ask for. When we pray "amiss," out of our own lusts and desires, we don't get what we ask for. We must pray in the nature of Jesus, and God's answer to those prayers is always yes and amen.

Let me encourage you to pray the Scriptures for yourself, your family, your nation, and the world. God has a perfect will for all of us and his perfect will is in his perfect Word. Here are a few verses to get you started.

> First of all, then, I urge that entreaties and prayers, petitions and thanksgivings, be made on behalf of all men, for kings and all who are in authority, so that we may lead a tranquil and quiet life in all godliness and dignity. This is *good* and *acceptable* in the sight of God our Savior, who desires all men to be saved and to come to the knowledge of the truth. 1 Timothy 2:1–4

Pray: *Thank you Father that is your desire that all men be saved and that all come to a saving knowledge of the truth. The sum of your Word is truth, absolute truth. Jesus Christ is the Way, the Truth, and the Life. Your Holy Spirit is the Spirit of Truth. Help us as a family and as a nation to come to the knowledge of the truth in all we are and in all we have been called to do.*

Thank you for those You have sovereignly chosen to be in authority over us in our jobs, our churches, our communities, cities, states, and in this whole great nation. We pray for your wisdom and guidance in their lives and in the decisions they make concerning us. What a blessing it would be to lead tranquil, quiet lives, in all godliness and dignity. Our nation needs this, our families need this. Help us Father, in Jesus' name.

There was no day like that before it or after it, when the LORD listened to the voice of a man; for the LORD fought for Israel. Joshua 10:14

Father we pray again for our leaders, that their voices would be ones You would listen to, and that You would fight for us. Listen to fathers and husbands and businessmen, and politicians, and doctors, employers, and all who have authority over us. Help them follow You wholly, like Joshua, and may you hear them when they call, and may the **Lord** *fight for us.*

Marriage is to be held in honor among all, and the marriage bed is to be undefiled; for fornicators and adulterers God will judge. Make sure that your character is free from the love of money, being content with what you have; for He Himself has said, "I WILL NEVER DESERT YOU, NOR WILL I EVER FORSAKE YOU," so that we confidently say, "THE LORD IS MY HELPER, I WILL NOT BE AFRAID. WHAT WILL MAN DO TO ME?" Hebrews 13:4–6

Your prayer:

There is so much power in praying the Word. Remember that as you daily come to God in prayer, you are to pray His word back to Him. Memorize it, meditate on it, obey it, and watch God be faithful to watch over His Word, for the purpose of fulfilling it in your life and in all the earth. Praise the Lord!

I hope and pray that the Scriptures and stories of personal victories have encouraged your heart and have strengthened you toward intimacy with God.

God wants intimacy with you, and I believe that is what you want from Him. You want those moments of passion when His Spirit comes and you know that the Lover of your soul is speaking peace, peace, wonderful peace. You want to use your name to fill in the blank, being His Princess of Sacrifice.

And why not? Now you know what it takes! Listen to the great cloud of witnesses surrounding you. Trust God with all of your heart. Never lean on your own understanding. In all, absolutely all, of your ways, know Him deeply, and He will direct your whole life (Prov. 3:5–6).

So I held my hands toward heaven,
And He filled them with a store
Of His own transcendent riches,
Till they could contain no more.

And at last I comprehended
With my stupid mind and dull,
That God could not pour His riches
Into hands already full!

Hold Nothing Back! Let sacrificial obedience lead *you* into intimacy with *God*.